T0068822

FREE WILL

FREE WILL

FREE WILL
An Opinionated Guide

Alfred R. Mele

OXFORD
UNIVERSITY PRESS

Oxford University Press is a department of the University of Oxford. It furthers
the University's objective of excellence in research, scholarship, and education
by publishing worldwide. Oxford is a registered trade mark of Oxford University
Press in the UK and certain other countries.

Published in the United States of America by Oxford University Press
198 Madison Avenue, New York, NY 10016, United States of America.

© Oxford University Press 2022

CIP data is on file at the Library of Congress

ISBN 978-0-19-757423-2

DOI: 10.1093/oso/9780197574232.001.0001

9 8 7 6 5 4 3 2 1

Printed by Integrated Books International, United States of America

For my father—again

CONTENTS

CONTENTS

PREFACE

Do we have free will? This book is an opinionated guide through a philosophical maze that leads to an answer. The journey through the maze is meant to be accessible to a very wide audience—to anyone who is willing to think along with me as we move forward. No prior training in philosophy is presupposed. I'll describe various philosophical positions on free will and explore their pros and cons. And I'll make a case for the position I favor.

* * *

I wrote this book during my tenure of a joint grant from the John Templeton Foundation and the Fetzer Institute. The opinions expressed here are my own and do not necessarily reflect the views of the John Templeton Foundation or the Fetzer Institute. I am grateful to both for their support. For comments on a draft of the book, I am grateful to Mark Balaguer, Roy Baumeister, Lucy Randall, Jay Spitzley, and the students in my undergraduate course in the Philosophy of Action at Florida State University in 2021. Chapter 4 draws liberally from my "Chance, Choice, and Freedom," *The Philosophers' Magazine* 55 (2011): 61–65.

| GETTING STARTED

In writing this book, I made lots of decisions. I made decisions about topics to discuss, examples to use, chapter titles, and so on. How many decisions would you estimate you make on an average day? I have a friend who always eats the same thing for breakfast when she's at home—Raisin Bran. When she's home for breakfast, she doesn't need to decide what to eat; she simply goes with her habit. What about you? Do you decide what to eat for breakfast most mornings? Do you decide what clothes to wear most days? Are some of your decisions relatively trivial whereas others are deeply important to you?

You know where this is heading. You and I make lots of decisions, but do we make any of them *freely*—of our own free will? Some people say no. Others say yes. But before we answer yes or no we should ask ourselves what we mean by *free will*.

A quick note before we move on: Throughout this book I'll be drawing primarily on resources from philosophy, including thought experiments and philosophical arguments. But science has a lot to say about free will too. If you're interested in science-based arguments for the idea that free will is an illusion and in critiques of those arguments (often, science-based critiques), I can recommend another book of mine, *Free: Why Science Hasn't Disproved*

Free Will. As the title suggests, I believe that science leaves room for free will. But let's not get ahead of ourselves.

1. Why Do People Care about Free Will?

In January of 2010, I launched the four-year Big Questions in Free Will project. The project's main aim was to bring scientists—specifically, neuroscientists and social, cognitive, and developmental psychologists—together with philosophers to explore big questions about free will. The project also had a theological wing that explored questions about divine freedom and the possible bearing of a supreme being on human freedom. The project was funded by a $4.4 million grant from the John Templeton Foundation. In all, about fifty scientists, philosophers, and theologians were involved.

The TV series *Closer to Truth* took an interest in the project. A dozen of their half-hour episodes between 2012 and 2015 are about free will and feature participants in the Big Questions in Free Will project. The *Closer to Truth* group also made a ninety-seven-minute documentary on the project, available on YouTube. The last time I checked, its YouTube views totaled over 1.5 million.

So why is there all this interest in free will—not just among philosophers, scientists, and theologians, but among people in general? Why is free will sufficiently important or interesting to people that they tune in to TV shows featuring experts talking about it?

Part of the answer may be found in the value people place on its being up to them what they do. To put it differently, people value having significant control over what they do. Although different people conceive of free will differently, almost everyone seems to tie it to some kind of control over our actions. Reflect on your own conception or image of who you are, including how you function in the world—how you live your daily life. If you are like most readers of this book, your self-conception—your view of yourself as a person—includes an assumption of free will. You take yourself to have significant control over what you do. You assume that it is often up to you what to do. And even if you yourself balk at calling this an assumption that you have *free will*, at least it's in the ball-park of free will.

Philosophers traditionally link free will tightly to moral responsibility, asserting that a being that lacks free will (for example, a fruit fly) isn't morally responsible for anything and therefore deserves neither blame nor praise from a moral point of view. Probably, you take it to be an important fact about yourself that you are morally responsible for some of what you do. If so, and if these philosophers are right, free will is included in your self-image.

In principle, we can be morally responsible both for good behavior and for bad behavior. Some people place special importance on the negative side of moral responsibility—on deserving blame and punishment for bad behavior. I don't. And, for the record, justifying a system of punishment has never played any role at all in my thinking about free will. I mention this because some skeptics about free will claim that believers in free will are motivated by a concern to justify harsh systems of punishment.

2. Deciding

Deciding (or choosing) what to do is at the heart of the philosophical literature on free will. Deciding what to do is often viewed as the phenomenon in which free will plays its most fundamental role. If I freely decided to do something, I may proceed to do it freely. But my doing it may be free precisely because the action is the implementation of a freely made decision.

Let's understand deciding what to do as a momentary mental action of intention formation and as something that's always a response to uncertainty about what to do. According to this way of thinking, my deciding to work at home today (rather than at my university) was a momentary mental action of forming an intention to work at home today. My decision was preceded by some thinking about some pros and cons, but that thinking wasn't part of my actual act of deciding. And if that thinking had revealed to me a clear winner, I would have implemented that option without having to decide to do so. My intention to implement it would not have been formed in a *decision* to implement it.

We get lots of our intentions without having to make corresponding decisions. For example, when I get to my office door on a normal morning, I unlock it—which, of course, I intend to do at the time. But, because things are normal, I'm not at all uncertain about what to do and therefore have no need to make a decision to unlock it. If I had heard people shouting in my locked office, I would have paused to think about what to do. And I would have made a decision about that. My uncertainty about what to do would have called for a decision.

Back to my decision about where to work today. When I made that decision, I definitely had the sense that it was up to me where to work. The decision was mine to make, and I made it. But did I make it freely? Did I make it of my own free will? That depends on what *free will* means.

3. Two Conceptions of Free Will

We'll be seeing two different conceptions of free will again and again. A simple way to understand them is in terms of proposed sufficient conditions for doing something freely. We'll treat *free action* as the more basic notion in terms of which *free will* is to be defined. Free will, as we'll understand it, is just the ability to act freely. And keep in mind that deciding to do something is itself an action; it's a momentary mental action of intention formation.

Let's start with freely deciding to do something. Here's a proposal about that:

Proposal 1. If sane, unmanipulated people consciously make a reasonable decision to do something on the basis of good information and no one is pressuring them, they freely decide to do that thing.

Call the conception of free will at work in this proposal a *Straight* conception. The reason for this label will be revealed shortly. It's important to keep in mind that Proposal 1 is a proposed *sufficient* condition for deciding freely. Proposal 1 doesn't say, for example, that you can't make a free decision while being pressured by someone. Nor does it say that a decision has to be reasonable in order to be free, that all free decisions have to be based on good information, and so on. Proposal 1 is not framed in terms of what's *necessary* for deciding freely. It's a proposal about what is *enough* for a decision to be free.

What do we mean by a *necessary condition* for something? What's a necessary condition for being a bachelor, for example? It's a condition that an entity must satisfy in order to be a bachelor. Here's one necessary condition. The entity must be unmarried. But is being unmarried a sufficient condition for being a bachelor? No. A sufficient condition for being a bachelor is a condition such that anything that satisfies it is a bachelor. The little boy who lives across the street from me is unmarried, but he doesn't count as a bachelor. So being unmarried isn't sufficient for being a bachelor. (By the way, my cell phone is unmarried too, and it's not a bachelor.) Other necessary conditions for being a bachelor are being a person, being male, being of marriageable age, and never having been married. (I checked an online dictionary for that last condition.) Putting all the necessary conditions for being a bachelor together yields a sufficient condition for being a bachelor.

I should add that not every part of a sufficient condition for a particular person's being a bachelor has to be a necessary condition for being a bachelor. My friend Juan is a fun-loving, twenty-five-year-old man who enjoys dating and has never been married. That's a sufficient condition for Juan's being a bachelor. But not all of the condition's components are necessary conditions for being a bachelor. A person doesn't need to be twenty-five to be a bachelor. And the same goes for being fun-loving and enjoying dating.

Back to Proposal 1. Why does it count as a proposal about free will, even though the expression *free will* doesn't appear in it? Because we're assuming that free will is the ability to act freely and we're understanding deciding to do something as a mental *action*. With this assumption in place, if a person decides freely, that person has free will—or at least had it when making the decision. Why? Because anyone who acts freely was *able* to act freely. And free will is precisely that ability—the ability to act freely.

Some people regard Proposal 1 as too feeble to take us all the way to free decisions. That is, they claim that satisfying Proposal 1 is *not sufficient* for deciding freely. What's missing, they say, is a requirement that alternative decisions are open to the decision-maker in a specific way that I will try to shed some light on now.

Sometimes you would have decided differently from the way you did if things had been a bit different. For example, if you had been in a slightly better mood, you might have decided to donate $20 to a worthy cause instead of just $10. But this isn't enough for the kind of openness of options in decision-making that some people say is necessary for deciding freely—what we can call *deep openness*. What's needed is that more than one option was open to you, given everything as it actually was at the time—your mood, all your thoughts and feelings, your brain, your environment, and, indeed, the entire universe and its entire history. Having been able to have made a different decision if things had been a bit different is one thing; having been able to have made a different decision without there being any prior difference at all is another thing—a more demanding or deeper thing. Hence the label *deep openness*.

Discussions of a conception of free will that requires deep openness for free decision-making can quickly get very technical. I'll try to avoid technicality here. Yesterday, George's friends invited him to join them on a karaoke outing. George doesn't care much for karaoke, but he likes hanging out with his friends. After giving the matter some thought, he decided to accept their invitation. Now, imagine that time (and the whole universe, actually) could be rewound in something like the way you rewind a movie you are watching on your favorite media player. And imagine that after George makes his decision, time is rewound to a moment just before he decided to say yes. Everything is exactly the same as it was the first time through. But this time, what happens next—what happens when the "play" button is pressed—is that George decides to reject his friends' invitation. This is a way to picture deep openness and the associated conception of having been able to have decided otherwise than the way you did. If George had deep openness when he made his decision, then if time could be rewound again and again for just a few moments and then played forward, he would make different decisions in some of the "replays."

This brings us to the following proposal:

Proposal 2. If sane, unmanipulated people consciously make a reasonable decision to do something on the basis of good information, no one is pressuring them, and they were able to make an alternative reasonable decision, in a sense of *able* that requires deep openness, they freely decide to do that thing.

The conception of free will at work in Proposal 2 is what I'll call a *Mixed* conception. I'll have much more to say about it in subsequent chapters. Here, I'll point out that Proposal 2 is understated insofar as it doesn't actually say that deep openness is *necessary* for free decision-making. So there's more to a Mixed conception than Proposal 2 identifies. A Mixed conception includes the idea that deep openness is *necessary* for free will.

Why do I call this conception *Mixed*? Because it mixes deep openness into the ingredients of the other conception I described. And why do I call the other conception *Straight*? Because it's unmixed. Some people like their whiskey straight; others prefer it mixed with ice. We find something analogous in the sphere of free will. Deep openness is the ice.

4. My Take on Free Will

As you will have noticed, this is not just a guide to free will—it's an opinionated guide. So in addition to guiding you in a general way on the topic, I'll present my own take on free will. There are many books you can read to explain free will to you, but this one introduces the topic while also presenting my view of it in particular. It's a view I've developed over many years, and it's a distinctive one. Maybe by the time you reach the end of this book, it will be your view, too. Or maybe—even better—you'll go on from this introduction to work out an exciting view of your own.

There's a long-standing debate in philosophy about whether free will is to be understood in a Straight way or in a more demanding way. I don't take a stand one way or the other in that debate. I never have. This is unusual, to put it mildly, for a philosopher who has written as much about free will as I have. One thing I've tried to do is to develop both an attractive Straight conception of free will and an attractive Mixed conception of it. With those conceptions before us, we can ask such questions as the following:

Do people ever satisfy the conditions that a Straight view presents as sufficient for free will?

Are those conditions actually sufficient for free will? Or can a person satisfy those conditions and lack free will even so?

Do people ever satisfy the conditions that a Mixed view presents as sufficient for free will?

Are those conditions actually sufficient for free will? Or can a person satisfy those conditions and lack free will even so?

We'll explore these questions, along with many others, in what lies ahead.

My friend and erstwhile coauthor, Helen Beebee, in a book aptly titled *Free Will: An Introduction*, cautions that "a willingness to think hard" would certainly help her readers (p. xi). I should say that if you hope to get through the book you're reading now without thinking much, you'll be disappointed. I'll try to explain things as clearly as I can, often with the help of thought experiments that I predict will hold your interest and deepen your understanding of free will. But my main aim is to help you think through the issues for yourself (while also nudging you in my philosophical direction on some of the main issues). If you're philosophically inclined, which you probably are if you have read this far, thinking about these challenging questions will be the fun part. You may even find you like it so much that, for you, this is just the beginning of a much longer exploration of free will.

2 | FREE WILL
STRAIGHT UP

Several years ago, someone came to Tallahassee to interview me about free will. As I explained a Straight conception of free will to him, the interviewer grew increasingly upset. Eventually, he interrupted and exclaimed that what I was talking about just wasn't free will. Undaunted, I continued my explanation and then turned to a Mixed conception, which the interviewer liked much better. Maybe you'll find my explanation of a Straight conception upsetting too, and maybe not. Time will tell. (Incidentally, to the best of my knowledge, that interview never saw the light of day.)

1. A Visit to Uone

As you'll recall, a Straight conception of free will is associated with what I unimaginatively called *Proposal 1*. Here it is again:

> Proposal 1. If sane, unmanipulated people consciously make a reasonable decision to do something on the basis of good information and no one is pressuring them, they freely decide to do that thing.

Proposal 1 looks pretty good, at least initially. Indeed, you might think that satisfying the condition stated there involves even more than what's needed to make a free decision—to decide something of your own free will. Perhaps some free decisions are based on information that is less than good. Maybe we can make free decisions while being pressured by someone to do something. And so on.

So why do some people worry—or even insist, as that interviewer did—that the condition stated in Proposal 1 is not sufficient for deciding freely? Let's start by imagining a possible universe. Call it *Uone*. Uone began with a Big Bang. Shortly after the Big Bang, all the laws of nature fell into place. Let's say that they were all in place by *time t*. Here's another fact about Uone: its laws of nature are such that a complete snapshot description of Uone at time *t* together with a complete catalogue of these laws *entails* a complete list of everything that ever happens in Uone, including everything people in Uone ever do. Just to be clear, as I use the word *universe*, you and I, along with our thoughts and feelings and our hopes and dreams, are parts of the actual universe—and, of course, the same goes for the inhabitants of Uone; they're parts of that universe.

What do I mean by *entails*? One statement entails another when it's impossible, logically speaking, for the first statement to be true and the second one false. For example, to hark back to my friend Juan, *Juan is a bachelor* entails *Juan is not married*. It's impossible for the former statement to be true without the latter statement also being true. Juan can't be a bachelor while also being married. This doesn't mean that Juan can't be married period. In fact, I predict that someday he'll marry. It means only that he can't be married while also being a bachelor.

Sometimes, discussion of a particular entailment is made easier by giving the relevant statements labels. A statement that we'll dub *Enormous* is composed of a complete list of Uone's laws of nature together with a complete description of that universe at time *t*. Another statement—we'll call it *Tiny*—is a true statement about something Ann did in Uone yesterday, billions of years after time *t*. *Tiny* is the statement that, yesterday, Ann had a cheese and tomato sandwich for lunch and shared it with her friend Barack. Given the way Uone's laws of nature work, *Enormous* entails *Tiny*. It's impossible for *Enormous* to be true without *Tiny* also being true.

If you read chapter 1 (and possibly even if you didn't), you can see where this is heading. Some people claim that free decision-making depends on what, in chapter 1, I called *deep openness*, and deep openness is absent in Uone. Furthermore, the condition deemed sufficient for deciding freely in Proposal 1 can be satisfied by someone who lacks deep openness; it can be satisfied by people in Uone, for example.

A reminder is in order. What's needed for you to have deep openness when you make a decision is that more than one option is open to you at the time, given everything as it actually is at the time—your mood, all your thoughts and feelings, your brain, your environment, and, indeed, the entire universe and its entire history. Let's go back to the idea of rewinding time. Imagine that after Ann finishes her lunch, time is rewound to a point before she has decided what to eat and then the "play" button is pressed. In Uone, no matter how many times this is done, Ann always has a cheese and tomato sandwich for lunch and shares it with Barack. That's the way Uone works. That Ann does this is entailed by a complete list of Uone's laws of nature together with a complete description of that universe at the dawn of time. If Ann had deep openness, then if time could be rewound and played forward again and again, Ann's lunch would be different in some of the "replays."

Philosophers who take a Straight perspective on free will deny that free will requires deep openness. If they were to respond to my little thought experiment about Uone, they might say such things as the following. For all we know, the actual universe works just the way Uone does. Suppose that one day scientists discover that our universe does work exactly like Uone and the news is widely circulated. Would people give up on the idea that we have free will and everything that depends on it? Don't gratitude and resentment, for example, presuppose free will in those to whom we are grateful and those we resent for their bad behavior? Would we stop believing that we are right to hold people accountable for some of what they do? And doesn't accountability presuppose free will? How could a discovery in the esoteric depths of physics warrant changing our view of ourselves and others so radically?

Proponents of a Straight conception of free will also challenge the claim that deep openness makes a contribution to free decision-making and free action in general. If a sane, unmanipulated person consciously makes a reasonable decision to do something on the basis of good information and no one is pressuring him, what good would having deep openness do him, they may ask. If deep openness makes no contribution to free will, it certainly isn't required for free will.

In the end, whether you opt for a Straight conception of free will or some alternative conception is likely to involve a cost-benefit analysis. We'll be looking into costs and benefits of Straight and Mixed perspectives on free will as this book progresses.

2. A Tale about Diana and Ernie

I'm about to describe a thought experiment that is designed to shed light on Straight conceptions of free will and pose a challenge to them. It's based on a thought experiment I used in my book *Free Will and Luck*. There are many published reactions to that thought experiment in the scholarly literature on free will. I'm interested here in your own reaction to the version of it I'm about to present.

Diana, a goddess, inhabits a universe, Utwo, that works just the way Uone does. It is now January 1, 1990, on Earth in Utwo. From her knowledge of Utwo's laws of nature and of everything that is going on there at this time, Diana deduces that a terrible virus will plague the Earth in 2020. She would like to create a human being who invents an excellent vaccine for the virus and shortly thereafter, on December 15, 2020, decides to give the formula free of charge to various nonprofit organizations. Diana would also like the person who does this to be sane and unmanipulated and to make this reasonable decision consciously, on the basis of good information, and in the absence of pressure (thereby satisfying Proposal 1). On the basis of the knowledge that I attributed to her—the same knowledge that enabled her to deduce that the terrible virus will exist in 2020—Diana deduces that if she combines certain atoms in a certain way to create a certain zygote and implants the zygote in Mary Smith of Plains, Georgia, at noon on January 2, 1990, that zygote will develop into a man, Ernie, who invents an excellent vaccine for the virus and, on December 15,

2020, decides, in just the way she wants, to give it free to certain nonprofit organizations.

When she did the deduction I described, Diana also deduced everything else Ernie would ever do. She was able to do this because all truths about what Ernie would do were entailed by a true statement of all of Utwo's laws of nature and an accurate description of everything that was going on at the time she started thinking about her project on New Year's Day of 1990. After she implanted the zygote in Mary, Diana turned her mind to other things. She never interfered with Ernie; she knew that she would have no reason to do that. By the way, Diana doesn't count anything she does as *manipulating* Ernie. After all, Ernie doesn't even exist when she creates the zygote and implants it in Mary. And even a goddess can't manipulate something that doesn't exist.

As I mentioned, Ernie satisfies Proposal 1 when he makes his decision. He does what a Straight conception of free will says is sufficient for deciding freely. But is it true that he makes his decision freely—that he makes it of his own free will? What's your view about that? Various philosophers have come down on different sides of this question regarding a very similar story about Diana and Ernie that I told in my book *Free Will and Luck*. And they would do so again regarding this version of the story. But my interest now is in your take on Ernie's decision.

Let's start with readers who believe that Ernie doesn't have free will when he makes his decision and, in fact, never has free will. Why might they think that? Well, they might observe that once the zygote is implanted in Mary, there's only one way for Ernie's life to unfold. Everything that Ernie will ever do is already in the cards at that point, they might say. And they might infer from this that it's never really up to Ernie what he will do and that he therefore lacks free will.

If these readers are right, Ernie's story is a counterexample to the claim that Proposal 1 provides a sufficient condition for deciding freely. Why? Because Ernie satisfies that condition when he makes his decision; and, if these readers are right, then despite satisfying this condition, Ernie doesn't decide freely. In short, if these readers are right, Ernie's story shows that Proposal 1 is false.

Here is an argument to consider. Let's call it *ZAF*.

ZAF

1. Ernie doesn't have free will.
2. Concerning free will of the beings into whom the zygotes develop, there is no important difference between the way Ernie's zygote comes to exist and the way any normal human zygote comes to exist in a universe with laws of nature like Utwo's.
3. So in no possible universe with laws of nature like Utwo's in which a human being develops from a normal human zygote does that human being have free will.

Statements 1 and 2 are *ZAF*'s premises, and statement 3 is its conclusion. Premises of arguments may be supported by other arguments. In fact, they should be supported by other arguments unless it's obvious that they are true. I have already indicated how someone might argue for *ZAF*'s first premise. What about its second premise?

By "an important difference" in *ZAF*'s second premise, I mean a difference that would support asymmetrical free will judgments about Ernie and some human being whose zygote comes to exist in the normal way in a universe with laws of nature like Utwo's. That is, the difference would support the judgment that Ernie lacks free will while also supporting the judgment that some human being of the latter kind has it.

Imagine a universe, Uthree, that is a lot like Utwo, in which a zygote exactly like Ernie's comes into being in Mary Smith of Plains, Georgia, in the normal way and at the same time as Ernie's does in Utwo. Uthree has the same laws of nature as Utwo. Throughout his life in Uthree, Mary's child, also named Ernie, does exactly what Ernie does in Utwo, down to the smallest detail, expressing values and motives that match those of the other Ernie. Might Uthree's Ernie have free will even though Utwo's Ernie doesn't? I suggested that someone who judges that Utwo's Ernie lacks free will may support that judgment by observing that once the zygote is implanted in Mary, there's only one way for Ernie's life to unfold. If that is true, it's also true that once Ernie's normally generated zygote comes to exist in Uthree, there's only one way for his life to unfold. (Keep in mind that Utwo and Uthree have the same laws of nature.) Add to this the following points: neither Ernie has any say about what causes his zygote to exist, nor does he have any say about anything going on in his universe when his zygote comes to exist, nor any say about what the laws of nature are in his universe. Given all this, it's plausible that the difference between the two Ernies—that one was the product of design and the other was not—doesn't support asymmetrical judgments about whether they have free will. That is, *ZAF*'s second premise is plausible.

I said twice now that some readers might observe that once the zygote is implanted in Mary, there's only one way for Ernie's life to unfold. This observation is correct, if what is meant is that a complete list of Utwo's laws of nature together with a complete description of that universe when the zygote is implanted entails all the facts about how Ernie's life unfolds. But I don't want to mislead you. Long before Diana created Ernie's zygote—indeed at the dawn of time in Utwo—a complete list of Utwo's laws of nature together with a complete description of that universe at that early time entails all the facts about how Ernie's life unfolds. And the same goes for Diana's life. If you like the *already in the cards* metaphor, we can say that way back then, it was already in the cards that Diana would create a zygote and implant it in Mary, that there would be a horrible pandemic in 2020, that Ernie would invent a vaccine, and so on.

We've been discussing how readers who reject the claim that Ernie has free will in the Diana and Ernie story might think about argument *ZAF*. What about readers who believe that Ernie does have free will in that story? What might they think about *ZAF*?

ZAF starts with a premise about Ernie in Utwo (designed Ernie)—namely, that he lacks free will. Its second premise is what we can think of as a *no-difference* premise. It implies, for example, that as far as free will goes, there's no important difference between designed Ernie and Uthree's Ernie. A reader who rejects the first premise might recommend that we open our reflections about *ZAF* by thinking about Ernie in Uthree. Imagine that the Ernies are thoughtful, considerate guys who care deeply about their families and friends and, indeed, about people in general. And imagine that they are sane and rational and make many thoughtful, reasonable decisions while not being pressured by anyone.

Now home in on Ernie in Uthree (who does all the same things as designed Ernie, as I mentioned). He has invented the vaccine and he's thinking about whether to make some money on it or instead to give the formula away for no gain to him. He believes that it would be morally permissible to make some money on it and generous to give it away. In the end, in the absence of external pressure and manipulation of any kind, he decides to give it away. This, an opponent of *ZAF* might say, is all one can reasonably ask of a free decision.

A reader who takes this position may be inclined to offer the Reverse *ZAF* argument—or *RZAF*, for short. Here it is:

RZAF

1. Uthree's Ernie has free will.
2. Concerning free will of the beings into whom the zygotes develop, there is no important difference between the way Ernie's zygote comes to exist in Uthree and the way designed Ernie's zygote comes to exist in Utwo; and both Ernies do all the same things, for the same reasons, and under the same conditions.
3. So designed Ernie has free will.

Readers who advocate *RZAF* may ask advocates of *ZAF* why they should regard the latter argument as more convincing than the former.

Here is Proposal 1 again: If sane, unmanipulated people consciously make a reasonable decision to do something on the basis of good information and no one is pressuring them, they freely decide to do that thing. The conception of free will at work here is what I called a *Straight* conception. Readers who are attracted to such a conception of free will may find *RZAF* persuasive. They may also find it useful as a tool for hitting the ball back into their opponents' court. Rather than claiming that *RZAF* is convincing, they may simply ask why *ZAF* should be regarded as more convincing.

3. Some Philosophical Terminology

Thus far in this chapter, I've been discussing a familiar issue in philosophy—the bearing of *determinism* on free will—without using the standard terminology. I did this for a reason. Part of the reason is that using the term *determinism* when discussing the issue—even when one carefully defines the term—can bias readers against a Straight conception of free will. As some readers understand *determinism*, it doesn't mean much more than *something that precludes free will*. And that's not what philosophers mean by it. I hoped that by discussing the idea at some length before using the term, I would mitigate the bias.

In mainstream philosophical writing about free will, we say that determinism obtains in a universe if a complete description of the universe at any time together with a complete list of all its laws of nature entails everything else that's true about the universe, including everything that will ever happen. And if a universe has people in it, among the things that happen in it are things that people do, including any decisions they make. I've already explained entailment to you; so you have the picture. Determinism obtains in Uone, Utwo, and Uthree. That is, as we philosophers put it, those universes are *deterministic*. To say that a universe is deterministic isn't to say that it *resembles* or *approximates* a universe in which determinism obtains. It's to say that it *is* a universe in which determinism obtains. (To say that a universe is *indeterministic* is simply to say that determinism does not obtain in it.)

You'll recall that when I described Uone, I said that all its laws of nature fell into place shortly after the Big Bang. This reflects one way of thinking about laws of nature—the way that is most common these days in philosophical writing about free will. But there are other ways. Laws of nature can be thought of as patterns of a certain kind that emerge over time and are less fundamental aspects of reality than the events in which the patterns are exhibited.

There's a label for philosophers who maintain that free will can exist in a universe in which determinism obtains. They're called *compatibilists*, and the position they propound is called *compatibilism*. (They have what I called a *Straight* conception of free will.) There's also a name for philosophers who maintain that compatibilists are wrong about this. They're called *incompatibilists*, and their position is called *incompatibilism*. (Many of them have a Mixed conception of free will.) Incompatibilists who believe that free will exists are called *libertarians*; they advocate *libertarianism*. This kind of libertarianism is to be distinguished from political libertarianism. They are two very different things. I'll be using these traditional labels from time to time in subsequent chapters.

3 | ALTERNATIVE POSSIBILITIES

At 7:00 this morning, Ann decided to have Wheaties for breakfast. According to the Principle of Alternative Possibilities—or one version of it, at any rate—Ann *freely* decided to do that only if, at that time, it was open to her to do something else instead. This principle can be formulated as follows:

> *PAP (for acting freely).* A person did something, *x*, freely at a time only if, at that time, it was open to her or him to do something other than *x* instead.

This principle is a proposed necessary condition for acting freely. Ann satisfies that condition if, for example, it was open to her at 7:00 to decide instead to have cornflakes or even just to think a bit longer about what to eat for breakfast.

Proponents of Straight and Mixed conceptions of free will who endorse this principle disagree about how to interpret it. The former interpret the principle in such a way that the required openness can be present in deterministic universes (as determinism was characterized toward the end of chapter 2), and the latter reject any such interpretation. There's a lot to be said about this disagreement and about whether the principle is true or false.

I framed the Principle of Alternative Possibilities in terms of something having been *open* to a person at a time. The principle can also be framed in terms of what a person was *able* to do at a time or what a person *could have* done at a time. These different ways of framing it come to the same thing. (Now that I've said that, I should point out that some philosophers think we're able to do something only if we're able to do it *intentionally*, so that we aren't *able* to do some things that we *can* do—for example, roll double sixes the next time we roll a normal pair of dice. I don't use the word *able* in that restrictive way. I just now took a break, tossed a pair of dice (just once), and happened to roll double sixes; and, as I use the word *able*, I couldn't have rolled double sixes just then if I hadn't been able to do that. Being able to do something intentionally is different from simply being able to do it.)

1. Frankfurt-style Stories

Frankfurt-style stories receive a lot of attention in philosophical discussions of free will. They are named after Harry Frankfurt, the author of a landmark journal article published in 1969. Although these stories tend to be strange, they are thought-provoking; reflection on them can be very fruitful. Frankfurt's article revolutionized thinking about free will and moral responsibility. It persuaded many philosophers that the Principle of Alternative Possibilities is false, and Frankfurt-style stories were used by some philosophers to bolster compatibilism. If the problem determinism poses for free will is that determinism seems to preclude the alternative possibilities needed for acting freely and alternative possibilities aren't actually needed for this, the problem vanishes.

The principle Frankfurt explicitly sought to undermine in that landmark article was about moral responsibility. But there is a parallel principle about acting freely. And because this book is about free will, we'll focus on the latter. By the *Principle of Alternative Possibilities* in this chapter, I always mean the principle that I formulated for you—that is, *PAP (for acting freely)*.

Let's start with a Frankfurt-style story that isn't particularly strange. It's about a pair of philosophers.

Beth ran into an old friend, Ann, at a philosophy conference. Philosophy professors love to talk about philosophy, and Beth and Ann were having a hard time hearing each other in the crowded hotel lobby. So they went up to Beth's room to continue their discussion. As it happens, they were talking about Frankfurt-style stories. After an hour or so, it occurred to Beth that Ann might want to go back downstairs. So she asked. Ann said she was finding the discussion thoroughly enjoyable and would much prefer to stay put and continue it. Beth replied that she felt exactly the same. They wound up talking there happily for another couple of hours.

As it turns out, another friend, Carlos, had locked the door to Beth's room from the outside shortly after Beth closed it. Ann and Beth didn't know it, but they hadn't been able to leave the room for quite some time. Even so, didn't they stay in the room of their own free will, happily discussing philosophy during that time? That is, didn't they stay there of their own free will *even though they couldn't have left*? If so, it looks like people can do something freely without being able to do otherwise, in which case the Principle of Alternative Possibilities is false.

Now, quick thinker that you are, you might say something like the following. Yes, they stayed in the room of their own free will. But they stayed there because they *decided* to do that. They made that decision of their own free will. And they could have decided otherwise. (Of course, if they had decided otherwise, they would quickly have discovered that the door was locked.) That they stayed of their own free will actually depends on their doing something when they could have done otherwise—namely, deciding to stay in the room.

This line of reasoning may be challenged. Suppose we change the story a bit: Ann and Beth were so engrossed in their conversation that they didn't even think about leaving the room and didn't make any decision about whether or not to leave. Eventually, Carlos came back, unlocked the door, and blamed the two women for spoiling his practical joke. Didn't they stay in the room of their own free will during their discussion, even though they made no decision of the kind at issue?

Is there an interesting way to avoid arguing about how to answer the question I just raised? Can we move the locked room into Beth's head, as it were, where any decision-making happens? This is where Frankfurt-style stories get strange.

Let's look at a relatively simple version of my favorite Frankfurt-style story (from an article by Dave Robb and me [1998]). It's set way off in the future at a time when there are experts at what's called *neuromanipulation*. A skilled neuroscientist named Harry would like Mary to decide at noon tomorrow to play a certain prank on Tarik later that day. The prank is to get the keys to Tarik's car, move it to another parking lot at their university, and then secretly put his keys back where she found them. While Mary sleeps in Harry's lab, Harry tinkers with her brain in such a way as to set in motion a process that is designed to cause her, at noon on the following day, to decide to pull this prank on Tarik. Mary doesn't know anything about this. And Harry is very confident that his tinkering will work exactly as planned. He has a perfect—and very lengthy—record at such manipulation.

Harry doesn't know it, but Mary had already been toying with playing this very prank on Tarik, a colleague of hers. Another thing Harry doesn't know is that the process he initiated will be preempted if Mary happens to decide on her own at noon to pull the prank. Shortly before noon, two relevant processes are still up and running in Mary. One is the process that Harry initiated last night, a process Mary is not conscious of. The other is Mary's own conscious thinking about what to do. The latter process, which is not affected in any way by the process Harry initiated, may or may not result at noon in a decision to pull the prank; whether it does or not is undetermined. But if Mary's conscious thinking about what to do does result at noon in that decision, Harry's process does not cause the decision. That's the only way the process initiated by Harry can fail to cause at noon the decision to pull the prank, if that process is still up and running at noon. And lo and behold, Mary decides on her own at noon to pull the prank on Tarik! Harry's process was preempted at that point.

As noon draws near, there are only two ways things can go for Mary. Either she decides at noon to pull the prank because Harry's tinkering caused her to make that decision then, or she decides on her own at noon to pull the prank—as a result of her own conscious thinking about what to do, and not because of anything Harry did. Either way, Mary decides at noon to pull the prank. If

Harry's tinkering had caused Mary to make the decision she made, then Harry would have forced her to make that decision and the decision would be unfree. But that's not what happened. Mary's decision was not caused by Harry. She made it on her own.

Assume for the sake of argument that there are lots of free actions—including many free decisions—in Mary's universe. Did Mary make her decision freely—of her own free will? What do you say?

Here's one way to think about it. Harry's neuromanipulation played no role at all in causing Mary's decision. As far as what causes Mary's decision goes, it's as though Harry did nothing at all. So take Harry out of the story. Now we have a much simpler story: Harry never interacts with Mary, and Mary decides at noon, on the basis of her own conscious reasoning, to play the prank on Tarik. Add that Mary is sane, that her decision is rationally made, and that there's nothing defective in the information she considers when thinking about what to do. With Harry out of the story, Mary's decision looks like a free one. So put Harry back in the story. Given that his tinkering played no role in producing that decision, how can putting Harry—and his tinkering—back in the story change Mary's decision from a free one to an unfree one? One answer is that it can't.

It's also helpful to have a look at my tale about Harry and Mary from the perspective of moral responsibility. Put yourself in Tarik's shoes. After work, you walk to where you parked your car, and it's not there. Your first thought—a very reasonable one—is that your car has been stolen. So you call the police, wait an hour or so for them to arrive, and spend a lot of time answering questions and then filling out paperwork. You miss the visit to the pub that you had been enthusiastically anticipating. After you finally fall asleep, too tired for thoughts about your car to keep you awake any longer, Mary calls to tell you where she parked it. She's laughing, and you're furious. You tell her that the prank wasn't funny at all. You say that it was downright nasty. And you definitely blame her for what she did.

Suppose Harry's boss phones you a bit later and informs you about two things—the tinkering Harry did, and the fact that the tinkering had no effect at all on what Mary decided to do (and then did) because she decided on her own to pull the prank. (The boss was worried that you or Mary would find out about the neuromanipulation without knowing the whole story and sue his company.) Now that you know this, do you believe that Mary has a good excuse for deciding to pull her prank and does not deserve to be blamed for deciding to do that? I strongly doubt it. After all, she made that decision on her own. Harry had no influence on it. If Mary does deserve to be blamed for her decision, did she make it freely? It would seem so. How can she deserve to be blamed for that decision if she made it unfreely? Her making it unfreely would get her off the hook.

At noon, could Mary have done otherwise than decide then to pull the prank? No. As I reported, at noon, there are only two ways things can go for her, and both involve her deciding then to pull the prank. Either she decides that on her own, or she decides that because Harry's neuromanipulation caused her to decide to pull the prank. So, at noon, Mary could not have done otherwise than decide to pull the prank. And even so, I predict that many readers have judged by now that she made her decision freely—of her own free will. After all, as you know, Harry's tinkering had no effect at all on Mary's decision. If you fall into this predicted group, you have what you can use as a counterexample to the Principle of Alternative Possibilities, as formulated above. Here's that principle again:

PAP (for acting freely). A person did something, *x*, freely at a time only if, at that time, it was open to her or him to do something other than *x* instead.

Why is this important? Well, for one thing, some people reject Straight conceptions of free will on the grounds that they can't accommodate the Principle of Alternative Possibilities. If you have a successful counterexample to this principle, the principle is false. And if the principle is false, no one needs to accommodate it.

This might be a good time to take a break. If you have a car and can't see it from where you are, you might like to check on whether it's still where you parked it.

OK. Now that you've had some time to think, you may have an urge to toy with alternative versions of the Principle of Alternative Possibilities. Perhaps Harry could have changed his mind after he neuromanipulated Mary. And perhaps, if he had changed his mind early enough, he would have been able to stop the process before noon. In that case, the following version of the principle survives the story of Harry and Mary: A person did something freely at a time *t* only if, *at some time*, a future in which she or he did something else instead at *t* was open to her or him. If Harry could have stopped the process at issue before noon, then (other things being equal) there was *some time* when a future was open to Mary in which she doesn't decide at noon to pull her prank and does something else at noon instead. Of course, once the modified principle is on the table, we may ask whether it's true or false. And one question that may quickly come to mind is how it can matter that Harry could have stopped the process that he initiated, given that that process had nothing to do with why Mary decides at noon to pull the prank. It is also worth mentioning that the story can be augmented with the detail that Harry can't change his mind. (Maybe someone else manipulated Harry!)

2. A Moral of Frankfurt-style Stories

Some people enjoy reflecting on Frankfurt-style stories. Others are put off by their strangeness. In any case, it's time to think about what morals may be drawn from them.

Consider the following two statements:

F1. Ann did x, and she wasn't forced to do that.

F2. Ann did x, and she could have done something else instead.

Normally, statements of these two kinds go together very nicely. On Monday, as Ann approaches a fork in the hiking trail, she decides to go left, but she could have decided to go right instead. From this, we infer that Ann wasn't forced to decide to go left. On Tuesday, as Ann approaches the same fork, she again decides to go left, and she wasn't forced to do that. Should we infer that she could have done something else instead—for example, decide to go right or decide to turn around? Well, we've just been discussing Frankfurt-style stories; and if this is one, then although Ann wasn't forced to decide to go left, she couldn't have done otherwise than make that decision.

These considerations may be taken to suggest that your having been able to do otherwise than you did is not crucial in its own right for free will and that its importance for free will lies in something it implies—that you *weren't forced* to do what you did. That is a potential moral of Frankfurt-style stories that goes beyond undermining the Principle of Alternative Possibilities.

Let's pursue this potential moral for a while. The basic idea is that your having been able to do otherwise than you did *isn't itself* a necessary condition for doing that thing freely but instead implies something that is necessary for acting freely—namely, that you weren't forced to do what you did. What's important here for doing x freely is that you weren't forced to do x. And if some Frankfurt-style stories work, there are possible scenarios in which you aren't forced to do what you did even though you couldn't have done otherwise.

As I mentioned early in this chapter, proponents of a Straight conception of free will who endorse the Principle of Alternative Possibilities interpret it in such a way that the required openness can be present in deterministic universes (as determinism was characterized toward the end of chapter 2), and proponents of a Mixed conception who endorse this principle reject any such interpretation. If the principle is false, this controversy's importance is diminished. But there's a related disagreement about what counts as a forced action.

Some readers may be inclined to believe that whenever people act in any deterministic universe, they are forced to do what they do. And others will disagree. It's time to look into this disagreement.

Recall that determinism obtains in a universe if a complete description of the universe at any time together with a complete list of all its laws of nature entails everything else that's true about the universe, including everything that will ever happen. Recall, too, that if a universe has people in it, among the things that happen in it are things that people do, including any decisions they make. Can there be both forced and unforced actions in a deterministic universe? Compatibilists say yes. An often-used example of a forced action is a compulsive hand-washer's washing his or her hands under the influence of an irresistible urge or compulsion to do so. The urge forces or compels the action. Another example is handing over the money in your pocket to a band of armed robbers. It is said that the robbers compel you to give them your money. (Some people say that we can refuse and fight. That would seem to depend on the psychological constitution of the person being threatened.) The great majority of human actions differ from these forced actions in obvious ways. Compare the compulsive hand-washer's behavior with my own hand-washing. (I'm normal in this connection, I assure you.) Compare the robbery victim's behavior with my giving some money to a homeless person asking for a few dollars. My behavior in this pair of circumstances certainly feels unforced, and compatibilists say that the accuracy of this feeling does not depend on whether our universe is or is not a deterministic one. Even if our universe is deterministic, they say, there's an important difference between compulsive hand-washers when they wash their hands and me when I wash mine.

Let's return to Proposal 1, a compatibilist proposal.

Proposal 1. If sane, unmanipulated people consciously make a reasonable decision to do something on the basis of good information and no one is pressuring them, they freely decide to do that thing.

During the COVID-19 pandemic, I did more hand-washing than usual. I didn't simply rely on my former habits to dictate whether I would or wouldn't wash my hands. Sometimes I thought about whether or not to do it, and I made a decision. Zoom in on, say, the tenth occasion on which I decided to wash them during the pandemic. In my opinion, I satisfied the condition set out in Proposal 1. And the same can't be said of many decisions about hand-washing made by compulsive hand-washers. Many of those decisions were *not reasonable*. Proposal 1 yields the result that my decision was free, but it doesn't yield the same result for a compulsive hand-washer.

Now consider the last time I decided to give a few dollars to a homeless person. That decision, in my opinion, satisfied Proposal 1. Compare this to a decision my friend Jay made to give the few dollars in his pocket to a knife-wielding robber. Jay is a large, powerful young man, and he briefly considered resisting. But he decided to hand over the money. Jay didn't satisfy Proposal 1. The robber was *pressuring* him.

Proposal 1's opponents can grant that, for some purposes, we can distinguish between my decision about hand-washing and a compulsive hand-washer's decision about that and between my decision to give some money to a homeless person and Jay's decision.

But, they will contend, the distinctions made are not about free versus unfree actions. To get to free action, they claim, we have to go further, and one thing we need is that the universes at issue are not deterministic.

An opponent of Proposal 1 can even grant that we can distinguish between forced and unforced actions in deterministic universes and then go on to claim that even unforced actions are unfree if determinism obtains in the universe at issue. If some Frankfurt-style story hits its mark, these opponents are not in a position to argue for their claim by appealing to the alleged requirement that free agents are able to do otherwise (as they interpret this ability). But they have other resources. If you look back at argument *ZAF* (about the zygote story) in chapter 2, you'll see that it doesn't explicitly appeal to this alleged requirement. In the following section, we'll consider another line of argument against Proposal 1 that doesn't explicitly appeal to this alleged requirement.

3. The Consequence Argument

Here's Peter van Inwagen's short formulation of an argument that lies at the heart of his much-discussed book, *An Essay on Free Will*. It is known as the Consequence Argument.

> If determinism is true, then our acts are the consequences of the laws of nature and events in the remote past. But it is not up to us what went on before we were born, and neither

is it up to us what the laws of nature are. Therefore, the consequences of these things (including our present acts) are not up to us. (p. 56)

To connect the quoted argument explicitly to free will, we can add the following premise:

P. If no actions of ours are up to us, then we lack free will.

And with this premise in place, we can draw the following conclusion:

C. If determinism is true (that is, if our universe is deterministic), then we lack free will.

If this conclusion is true, then Proposal 1 is false. You know why by now. Proposal 1 is satisfiable in a deterministic universe. That is, the conditions that Proposal 1 presents as being sufficient for freely deciding to do something—and therefore, for having free will—can be met in a deterministic universe.

A key notion in the Consequence Argument is something's being *up to* someone. What does that involve? In what I just quoted, van Inwagen says that if determinism is true, "our present acts . . . are not up to us." As I said, what I quoted is a short formulation of the Consequence Argument. His discussions of longer formulations make it clear that he's thinking that an action of yours was up to you only if you could have done otherwise. Now, if some Frankfurt-style story hits its mark, a person can freely do something, *x*, even though he couldn't have done otherwise than *x*. Suppose that some Frankfurt-style story does hit its mark. And suppose that an action a person performed—say, Mary's deciding to play a certain prank on Tarik—counts as up to that person only if she could have done otherwise than decide to play that prank. The upshot of this pair of suppositions is that a person can do something freely—and therefore have free will—even though that action wasn't up to her. And that upshot contradicts premise P, the premise I added to connect the short version of the Consequence Argument explicitly to free will. Do you think the two suppositions are true? If so, you probably think that the Consequence Argument ought to be rejected. We'll return to this point at the end of this section.

The point I just made about premise P raises an interesting question. Can we find a reading of *up to me* according to which an action can be up to me even though I couldn't have done otherwise? Attention to a conversation I had with my friend Marcela a while ago might help. She asked me where I'd like to have lunch later in the day, and I said, "It's up to you." What did I mean? Something like this, I believe: Marcela can decide, and I'll go along with her decision. That use of *up to* doesn't commit me to thinking that, whatever Marcela decides, she could have decided (or *could have done*) otherwise. Marcela replied, "No, it's up to you," and I said, "OK." What did I mean by that? Something like this: "I'll decide where to have lunch and Marcela will come along." I took myself to have different options, but I didn't need to believe that those options were consistent with the combination of the laws of nature and a complete description of the universe at some point in the remote past. Substitute my friend Stevie for me. He believes that determinism is true and he makes lots of decisions. The options he considers when he does so are ones that, *for all he knows*, are consistent with this combination—even if at most one of them is actually part of a possible continuation of the past, given the laws of nature.

Given what I have said thus far, how might we understand a sentence like this: "It's up to me where to have lunch"? We might try this: "I can decide where to have lunch and then have lunch there." This doesn't entail that I can do otherwise. But what about a sentence like the following: "What I *decide* about where to have lunch is up to me"? What does that mean? Maybe this: "I'm in control of what I decide about where to have lunch." If we take this to entail that I could have decided otherwise than I did, and if we think that some Frankfurt-style story works, we don't want to claim that being in control of what one decides is a necessary condition for deciding freely. But must we take the sentence at issue to have this entailment? Maybe all it means is this: I will decide where to have lunch and nothing will force me to decide as I do.

We have come back to the issue that I used to set the stage for the present section. Are all actions unfree if determinism obtains, including unforced actions? The Consequence Argument, given the present reading of *up to*, leaves us where we were. So let's set Frankfurt-style stories aside for a while and take another look at the Consequence Argument. Here it is again, in a slightly different form.

The Consequence Argument (Again)

1. If determinism is true, then our acts are the consequences of the laws of nature and events in the remote past.

2. It is not up to us what went on before we were born, and neither is it up to us what the laws of nature are.
3. Therefore, the consequences of these things (including our present acts) are not up to us.
   P. If no actions of ours are up to us, then we lack free will.
   C. Therefore, if determinism is true (that is, if our universe is deterministic), then we lack free will.

Whatever may be meant by *up to us*, we may grant that we had no control at all over what happened before we were born and no control at all over what the laws of nature are while also supposing, for the sake of argument, that our universe is deterministic. But this wouldn't commit us to concluding that we have no control over anything. When I drive my car around town, I control its movements in ways that my passengers don't. As I type this sentence, I control the motions of my hands and fingers. When I shoot pool, I control the movements of my cue stick. And so on. All this is true even if our universe is deterministic.

Among the kinds of control that people may have in deterministic universes, are any of them what may be called *free-will-level control*? On this question, compatibilists and incompatibilists have disagreed for millennia. Incompatibilists contend that this kind of control can't be had in any deterministic universe, and compatibilists deny that. I certainly won't be resolving this disagreement here. But what I can do is to present both positions to you for your consideration along with my own take on free will.

My discussion of the Consequence Argument here has been complicated. So what's the take-home message? The message has two parts.

Part 1. Suppose that an action I performed counts as up to me only if I could have done otherwise than perform that action. Then if some Frankfurt-style story works, it would show that an action doesn't need to be up to me in order for me to perform it freely, in which case the Consequence Argument would bite the dust. Now, the statement that I freely did something that wasn't up to me sounds odd. And if you find that sound unbearable, one option you have is to reject the supposition that an action of mine counts as up to me only if I could have done otherwise. If I'm a character in a Frankfurt-style story who decides on his own to do something (on the basis of good information and so on), you might see that as sufficient for my decision's having been up to me—even though I couldn't have decided otherwise.

Part 2. Our having no control over what happened before we were born and no control over the laws of nature doesn't entail that we have no control over anything that we do—even if our universe is deterministic. The Consequence Argument notwithstanding, it remains an open question whether the control people have over what they do in a deterministic universe is ever free-will-level control.

4. Being Able to Do Otherwise

One moral of Frankfurt-style stories—the main moral, in fact—is that freely doing x doesn't depend on being able to do otherwise than x. Because of the central place of Frankfurt-style stories in this chapter, I haven't said much about the idea, advocated by traditional compatibilists, that determinism doesn't preclude being able to do otherwise—or, at least, any kind of ability to do otherwise that is required for acting freely.

Consider Al driving to his office today, and imagine that his universe is deterministic. Al made a left turn at Macomb Street, as he often does. Could he have driven one block further and turned left at Copeland Street, as he sometimes does? (Usually, he continues driving west on Tennessee Street for the extra block if the left turn lane on Macomb is full.) Some traditional compatibilists point out that if Al had had a good reason to stay on Tennessee Street for another block, he would have done so, and they say that this sort of thing counts as being able to do otherwise. They're not saying that in some other possible universe with the same past as Al's deterministic universe and the same laws of nature, he drives to Copeland Street. They know that in any possible universe with the same past and laws of nature as Al's deterministic universe, he does the same thing. They're saying that being able to do otherwise—at least if we're talking about something required for free will—is a matter of being capable of adjusting one's behavior to one's reasons. And Al is capable of doing that. When traffic conditions are normal, he turns left at Macomb; and when he has a good reason to delay his left turn until he gets to Copeland Street, he adjusts his behavior and does that.

Of course, incompatibilists contend that this sort of thing isn't a genuine ability to do otherwise or that an ability to do otherwise, construed in this compatibilist way, falls short of the robust kind of ability we need in order to act freely. One thing that's required of an ability to do otherwise that does the work that needs to be done, they claim, is that it's an ability to do something (other than what one actually did, of course) that is a possible continuation of the actual past, given the laws of nature. Such an ability can be found only in indeterministic universes.

4 | A WHIRLWIND TOUR

Like that grumpy interviewer I mentioned in chapter 2, some readers may not have much enthusiasm—or even much patience—for a Straight conception of free will. They may be relieved to learn that we're moving on now to an alternative outlook on free will, a Mixed conception.

1. A Toy Model of Deep Openness

As we saw in chapter 1, a Mixed conception of free will is associated with the following proposal:

> Proposal 2. If sane, unmanipulated people consciously make a reasonable decision to do something on the basis of good information, no one is pressuring them, and they were able to make an alternative reasonable decision, in a sense of *able* that requires deep openness, they freely decide to do that thing.

You may recall that what's needed for you to have deep openness when you make a decision is that more than one option is open to you at the time, given everything as it actually is at the time—your

43

mood, all your thoughts and feelings, your brain, and your environment, along with the entire universe and its entire history. I hope you're not tired of the "replay" metaphor yet, because I'm going to use it again. Today, I thought about what to have for lunch and I decided on a cheese and tomato sandwich with a pickle on the side. I made that decision at noon. If I had deep openness at noon, then if time could be rewound to just a moment before I made my decision and then played forward, in some of the "replays" I would decide on one of the other options I was considering.

With these reminders in place, we can get to work on fleshing out a Mixed conception of free will. Proposal 2 is a proposed *sufficient* condition for free decision-making. What about *necessary* conditions? There's at least one thing that all proponents of a Mixed conception of free will agree is necessary for free decision-making (and for all free actions). It's that determinism, as characterized toward the end of chapter 2, does not obtain in the decision-maker's universe. That determinism does not obtain in a universe—that is, that the universe at issue is *indeterministic*, as we philosophers say—is required for there to be deep openness in that universe. But for decision-makers to have deep openness depends on more than simply that their universe is indeterministic. It requires that their universe is such that, on at least some occasions, at the time at which they made a decision, their doing something else instead right then (for example, making a different decision) is not precluded by a combination of their universe's laws of nature and everything that has happened in their universe up to that time.

Consider an indeterministic universe, Ufour, in which there are several planets that host advanced civilizations. There are governments, stock markets, sports teams, universities, and so on;

and there are billions of decision-makers. Some of their decisions are indeterministically caused by their proximate causes (that is, by the causes that immediately precede the decisions). What does that amount to? Suppose that, at midnight, Cathy decides to quit her job. Call the proximate causes of her decision to do that *PC*. PC may include a host of things, including her dissatisfaction with some of her employer's policies, her desire for a higher salary, and her belief that she can easily find a better job. To say that PC indeterministically causes Cathy's decision at midnight is to say two things. First, it causes her decision at midnight. (That's obvious!) And, second, the pertinent laws of nature in Ufour left open the possibility that PC would not cause that decision then. In another possible universe that's exactly the same as Ufour up to the moment at which PC causes Cathy's decision to quit her job, PC doesn't cause that decision. Perhaps Cathy decides instead at midnight not to quit yet. Or perhaps she keeps thinking about what to do for a while. These other outcomes in other possible universes have causes—including proximate causes—and the pertinent laws of nature leave open the non-occurrence of these options. We can say that laws of nature like this are *probabilistic* or *indeterministic*. They differ from the laws of nature in deterministic universes in that probabilistic or indeterministic laws are compatible with there being different possible continuations of the same past.

We'll be working with a Mixed conception of free will that requires deep openness for free decisions. We've already seen one way to picture deep openness—the "replay" way. In this section we'll see another.

You're enjoying a leisurely walk in the woods when you come to a fork in the path. You pause to think about what to do, and you decide to go left. According to some philosophers, if free will was at work at the time, you could have acted differently.

Philosophers tend to be cautious about theoretical matters. Deciding to go right is a different mental action from deciding to go left. But so is continuing to think about what to do (while remaining undecided). Other alternatives include deciding to turn back and deciding to sit for a while, among many others. The main point, according to the philosophers I have in mind, is that if you freely decided on the left fork, you could have done something else instead at the very time you made that decision.

What does the idea that you could have done something else at the time come to? According to some philosophers, it comes to this: in a hypothetical universe that has exactly the same past as our universe and exactly the same laws of nature, you do something else at this very time. In our universe, you decide on the left fork at noon. And in a possible universe that would have been actual if you had behaved differently at noon—one with the same past as the actual universe right up to noon and the same laws of nature—you do something else at noon. If this is how things are, you had what I called *deep openness* when you made your decision. The "replay" idea is designed to help you picture this.

Does deep openness fit your experience of decision-making, at least in some cases? I predict you'll say yes. I'm not saying that you experience other possible universes. The question is whether it sometimes seems to you that, when you decide to do something, you could have done something else instead—and not just in the sense that if the past (or the laws of nature) had been different, you would or might have done something else. Your answer, I'm guessing, is yes.

How do your decision-making processes work if and when you have deep openness? A simple model might help. Here's one. When you are unsettled about what to do, your beliefs, desires, wishes, hopes, habits, reasoning, and the like all feed into a tiny neural roulette wheel in your head. The wheel has a thousand slots. The slots represent outcomes. For example, two hundred slots may represent your deciding on the left fork at noon while another two hundred represent your deciding on the right fork then. Continuing to think at noon about which fork to take may be represented by five hundred slots. And the remaining hundred may be divided among such things as deciding to turn around, deciding to sit down, and so on. The number of slots assigned to any particular option reflects the probability that that option will be the outcome of this spin of the wheel. For example, if two hundred of the one thousand slots are assigned to your deciding on the left fork at noon, there's a 20 percent chance that that's what you'll do at noon. What determines the number of slots assigned to an option are the psychological factors I mentioned—your beliefs, desires, habits, and so on.

The wheel is activated by your uncertainty about what to do. When that happens, the wheel starts spinning and a tiny neural ball drops onto it. The ball bounces along the wheel and eventually lands in a slot. Its landing in a slot represents a mental action— for example, deciding to take the left fork or continuing to think about what to do. If it lands in a slot for your taking the left fork, let's say that its landing there *is* your deciding to go left. And the same goes for its landing in a slot for some other mental action; its landing there *is* that mental action (deciding to go right, for example, or thinking about what to do).

I'm not claiming that this is the only model of how you work as a decision-maker if and when you have deep openness. But it is a model, and it may help you think about the nature of deep openness. The model suggests that your deciding on the left fork at noon was partly a matter of luck. Until the ball settled into a slot for that decision, there was a chance that it would land in a slot for another mental action instead.

Deep openness can be frightening. Imagine an unstable president who believes it would be best not to order a nuclear attack but is considering doing it anyway, out of anger. He has deep openness, the launch button is in front of him, and pressing it is represented by several slots on his wheel. Pressing the button would probably start World War III, as the president knows.

You may prefer a less frightening story, as I do. Here's one. Joe is down on his luck. He was expelled from college for cheating a few weeks ago, and his parents disowned him. He's been struggling to make ends meet. Joe's complaints about his condition in a sketchy saloon prompt a stranger to offer to sell him a gun. "With this," the stranger says, "you can raise a lot of money in a hurry." Joe's wheel starts spinning. He has never committed a violent crime and he has never handled a gun, but he is open to the possibility. He decides to buy the gun. In another possible universe in which everything is the same right up to the moment he makes that decision, he decides to decline the offer.

A couple of days later, Joe's thoughts turn to the gun. He considers selling it for a small profit. His wheel starts spinning. Joe decides to keep the gun for a while, but he could have decided to sell it. If the ball had landed one slot away, that's what he would have done.

A week passes and Joe is wondering how he'll pay his rent. He thinks again about selling the gun. And again the wheel starts spinning. He decides to use the weapon at a small shop on the other side of town. Joe's plan is to brandish it while loudly demanding money. He's confident that the cashier will simply comply; he definitely has no intention of firing the gun. Unfortunately, things don't go according to plan. As Joe is speaking to the cashier in what he hopes is a very threatening voice, he sees the man reach under the counter—perhaps for a weapon. Joe thinks about running away, and his wheel is activated. He decides to fire a warning shot. But he's nervous and shaky. He accidentally shoots the cashier in the hand. Things could have turned out very differently.

We'll return to Joe shortly, after a brief note on brain science. Some scientists have reported what they regard as evidence of indeterministic brain processes that influence behavior. Indeterministic processes, by their nature, leave open more than one outcome. The experiments I have in mind were done with fruit flies, not human beings. But if tiny brains are indeterministic organs, that certainly suggests that big ones are too. The tiny neural roulette wheel is a cartoon image of how an indeterministic brain might work in producing decisions. I won't speculate about the low-level mechanics of indeterministic brain processes, but I will mention an alleged possibility. In his book *Mindful Universe*, Henry Stapp suggests that there are quantum probability clouds associated with calcium ions moving toward nerve terminals. This low-level openness (if it exists) can underwrite deep openness.

Back to Joe. He had a string of bad luck. He made several bad decisions. Joe definitely isn't a hardened criminal, and he's far from thoroughly bad. He's good enough to have decided not to buy the gun, to have decided to sell it without ever using it, and so forth. And, each time, if the ball had landed just a slot or so away, he would have made a better decision.

Does Joe's bad luck get him off the hook? Does it mitigate his moral responsibility for his bad decisions? Or what? These questions are difficult. Some reflection on Joe's internal workings might help.

In the roulette wheel model of deep openness, as you saw, a person's beliefs, desires, wishes, hopes, habits, reasoning, and so on all feed into the tiny wheel and determine what its slots represent (and how many slots a possible outcome gets). All these things are influenced by past decisions the person has made and his or her past behavior. People can and do learn from their mistakes and from their successes; and what they learn has an effect on how the wheel is divided up when it's time to make a decision. Efforts at self-improvement can also have an effect on this. A person who has been smoke-free for a year is likely to have a very different distribution of outcome slots when he feels tempted to smoke now than he did a year ago. The same is true of a person who has made a lot of progress in overcoming a tendency to procrastinate or overeat.

With this in mind, we might be inclined to see Joe as having significant responsibility for how his wheel is configured when he makes the decisions I described and for the decisions he ends up making. After all, he spent years shaping his wheel. To be sure, whenever there was deep openness in his decision-making, some luck (or chance) was involved—but *some luck* might not be enough to absolve him of responsibility entirely.

There are people who want to have their cake and eat it too. Some such people may want to have a kind of control over their decisions that includes deep openness and leaves nothing to chance. They may believe that only this kind of control—call it *Magic*—can make it truly up to them what they do. But this kind of control is just as impossible as a delicious cake sitting on my kitchen counter even though I just devoured the last piece. Why? Because indeterministic control in the absence of chance is impossible. If Joe decided with deep openness to buy the gun, there was, right up to the moment he made that decision, a chance that he would not make that decision then.

Some believers in Magic may be irresistibly drawn to the conclusion that Joe lacks free will and moral responsibility. But some of us seem to be free to struggle with the question of how free will and moral responsibility can coexist with deep openness. I tackle this question in my books *Free Will and Luck* and *Aspects of Agency*—even though I'm not convinced that free will requires deep openness. And I'll say something about this issue here.

Many games involve a mixture of luck and skill. In blackjack, players compete only with the dealer, whose every move is dictated by the rules. Unlike the dealer, the players have options: for example, they can hit (request another card), stand (refuse additional cards), double their bets in certain situations, and split pairs (for example, two aces) into two hands. What cards one gets is a matter of luck, and skilled players have memorized and are guided by reliable tables about when they should hit, stand, and so on. Very skilled players keep track of the cards they have seen—they "count cards"—and they adjust their strategy accordingly.

Free will may also involve a mixture of luck and skill. According to one way of thinking about free will, just as luck is an essential part of (legal) blackjack, the kind of luck involved in deep openness is an essential part of becoming a free agent. But whereas luck is an ineliminable part of legal blackjack, free agents might reasonably seek to eliminate (or at least reduce) luck in an important sphere of life. Blackjack players who want to maximize their chances of winning (legally, of course) should learn how to minimize the potential consequences of bad luck and to maximize the potential consequences of good luck. So they should learn to count cards, memorize a good set of blackjack tables, and play accordingly. What might rational folks do about the luck involved in deep openness, given their aspirations? One thing they might do is to try to become so good at resisting or avoiding temptation that there is no longer a chance that they will decide contrary to what they judge best. If you see no good reason to prefer the left path to the right, and vice versa, a wheel that gives you a 50 percent chance of each decision should be fine with you. But when you know that it would be much better to go left than to go right, a wheel that gives you a chance of deciding to go right is potentially dangerous.

Rational folks also try to learn from their mistakes and successes, and they sometimes embark on projects of self-improvement. Again, in the roulette wheel model of free agency, these efforts shape decision wheels.

In "Gimme Shelter," Mick Jagger warned that war is just a shot away. In a decision-maker with deep openness, war might be just a slot away. Fortunately, decision-makers who can shape their wheels are not entirely at the mercy of luck. And, with luck, perhaps free agents are able to configure their wheels in such a way that they have no chance at all of making very bad decisions.

2. Some Questions

The preceding section was a whirlwind tour of deep openness. In the next chapter, we'll slow down and look more carefully at some of the issues raised by the tour—either explicitly or implicitly. Does deep openness make a contribution to free decision-making? Is deep openness instead an obstacle to free decision-making? Framing things in terms of the decision-wheel model, does the bearing of people's past behavior on the present configuration of their decision wheels help us see how the preceding two questions should be answered? These questions set the agenda for chapter 5.

5 | MIXING IT UP

This chapter picks up right where chapter 4 left off. It's time to look more deeply into deep openness and its bearing on free will.

1. The Problem of Present Luck

We'll start with what I call *the problem of present luck*. Let's pick one of the decisions Joe made and examine it for signs of luck—bad luck, in Joe's case. His decision to commit the armed robbery will do.

Is Joe morally responsible for deciding as he did? Does he deserve to be blamed for deciding to rob the shop? Here's one way to think about the matter. If Joe had been just a bit luckier, he would have decided against the robbery. In another possible continuation of his universe's past (with no change in the laws of nature), that's exactly what happens. If the ball had landed just a couple of slots away, Joe would have decided not to rob the shop. Focus on two universes that are exactly the same right up to the moment at which Joe makes his decision. In one, he decides to rob the shop, and in the other he decides not to rob it. This difference between the two universes seems to come down to a difference in luck for Joe. And if that is so, does Joe have enough control over what he decides to deserve to be blamed for his bad decision?

Let's beef up the story a bit. In the beefed-up version, Joe does his best to resist his urge to rob the shop. He makes a concerted effort to get himself to do what he believes is right instead. He focuses on the possible unwanted consequences of a robbery, on the kind of person he wants to be, and the like. But in the end, he decides to rob the store. In another possible universe that's exactly the same right up to that point, Joe's efforts pay off; he decides instead not to commit the robbery. His efforts at self-control—like everything else up to the moment of decision—were exactly the same in both universes, but those efforts failed in one and succeeded in the other. Once again, it's easy to see Joe as not having enough control over what he decides to be morally responsible for his decision. In the universe in which he decides on the robbery, he seems to be a victim of bad luck.

Here's another way to put the worry about luck. If there is nothing about Joe's abilities, capacities, state of mind, moral character, reasoning, efforts at self-control, and the like in either universe that accounts for the difference in what he decides, then the difference seems to be just a matter of luck. And given that neither universe differs from the other in any respect at all before he makes his decision, there is no difference at all in Joe in these two universes to account for the difference in his decisions. To be sure, something about Joe may explain why it's *possible* for him to decide to rob the shop in one universe and to decide not to rob it in another universe with the same past and the same laws of nature. That he's an indeterministic decision-maker may explain this.

That's entirely consistent with the difference in his decisions being just a matter of luck. We may cite reasons for which Joe decides to rob the shop in one universe and reasons for which he decides not to rob it in another. But, of course, he has the same reasons for and against deciding on the robbery in both universes. Which reasons prevail seems to be at least partly a matter of luck. All things considered, then, we seem to be well within our rights to entertain doubts that Joe has enough control over what he decides to be morally responsible for his unfortunate decision.

Here's the connection to free will. Suppose that Joe's decision was indeed too much a matter of luck for him to be morally responsible for it. Well, if he made that decision of his own free will, he would be morally responsible for it. So the judgment that he isn't morally responsible for deciding to rob the shop leads in a straightforward way to the conclusion that he didn't make that decision freely. This is an illustration of the problem of present luck for proponents of a Mixed conception of free will. Now that we see the problem, what should we think about it? Some problems have solutions. Some don't. What about this one?

2. A Solution to the Problem of Present Luck?

Is there a solution to the problem of present luck? I believe so. But it isn't a simple one. So I'll ask you to bear with me as we work our way up to it.

In chapter 4, I intimated that when thinking about whether free will and moral responsibility can coexist with deep openness, we should attend to how a person like Joe came to be the way he was when he made one of the unfortunate decisions I described. This suggestion runs counter to a popular idea in the philosophical literature on free will and moral responsibility. Let's define your *internal condition* at a time, *t*, as something specified by the collection of all psychological truths about you at *t* that are silent on—that is, say nothing about—how you came to be as you are at *t*. We can think of this as a psychological snapshot of you at this time. The snapshot includes all of your current beliefs, desires, emotions, psychological tendencies, and the like. The popular idea is that if we have this snapshot to examine and we know how your internal condition at the time is related to what you do at the time, we have all we need to draw a correct conclusion about whether you acted freely and were morally responsible for what you did. For ease of reference, let's give this popular idea a name. Let's call it the *Snapshot View*.

In effect, I suggested that the Snapshot View is false and that, at least sometimes, it matters how people came to be in the internal condition they're in at the time of action—matters, that is, for whether their actions are free and whether they are morally responsible for those actions. Why does it matter? You're ready for part of the answer now.

Return to Joe and imagine that, for the past few weeks, around the time his serious problems started, how his decision wheel was configured during decision-making had nothing at all to do with his past behavior. During those few weeks, every time he was uncertain about what to do, something in his brain that worked like a random number generator—a genuinely indeterministic one—randomly produced assignments for all the slots on his decision wheel. Even though in the past, for good financial reasons, he almost always took a bus to his friend Jim's house for their weekly Netflix nights, the wheel might arbitrarily give him a 90 percent chance of deciding on an expensive taxi ride this time. Even though, given his financial situation, he had never decided on the high-priced peanut butter at the corner store, this time, without any difference in his financial situation, the wheel might randomly give him an 87 percent chance of rejecting the much cheaper generic peanut butter in favor of Jif. And so on—for every decision he makes. There's just one restriction on the random device: only things that Joe is capable of conceiving of doing at the time get a slot. In this scenario, during the few weeks at issue, we have the problem of present luck on steroids! Not only is it open which segment of the wheel the ball lands in, it also is entirely a matter of luck what the probabilities are for Joe's making various decisions or performing other mental actions and even what options are on the wheel (with the one exception I mentioned; no slots are assigned to things Joe can't conceive of doing at the time).

In this modified thought experiment about Joe, he certainly seems to be too much at the mercy of luck to be morally responsible for the decisions he makes during the few weeks at issue. Would he be better off in this regard if the configuration of his wheel depended significantly on decisions he made in the past, on his reflection on the consequences of some of those decisions, on his past efforts at self-improvement (if any), and the like?

It would be nice if we could take up this question right now. But once someone suggests, as I have done, that how Joe's decision wheel came to be configured as it is has an important bearing on whether or not he decides freely and is morally responsible for his decision, a question arises about a person's first free action or the first action for which a person is morally responsible. (Keep in mind that decisions are actions.) Since it's the (presumably very young) person's *first* free or morally responsible action that we're wondering about, it can't be influenced by any earlier such action performed by this person. So how do free will and moral responsibility get off the ground? This is the question that needs attention now.

If free will and moral responsibility exist, how do we get from being neonates, who don't even act intentionally, much less freely and morally responsibly, to being free, morally responsible people? And how might this happen on a Mixed conception of free will? In developing an answer, we'll focus on moral responsibility. If moral responsibility exists, we sometimes are morally responsible for things we don't freely do. For example, a drunk driver who is too drunk even to see the pedestrian he is about to run over and kill is morally responsible for killing the person even though the killing is a horrible accident and not something he does of his own free will. But the actions we'll be considering are of such a kind that the children performing them wouldn't be morally responsible for them if they weren't performing them freely.

Under normal conditions, parents eventually come to view their children as having some degree of moral responsibility for what they do. The word *degree* is important here. Normal five-year-olds are not as well-equipped for impulse control as normal ten-year-olds, and they have a less developed capacity for antici-pating and evaluating the effects of their actions. When normal five-year-olds snatch an appealing toy from a younger sibling's hands, most people take them to be morally responsible and blameworthy for that, but not as responsible and not as blameworthy as their normal ten-year-old siblings are for doing the same thing. (This is true at least of most people with a robust memory of significant dealings with children of these ages.) A simple way to account for this difference in how people regard these children is in terms of their grip on the fact that, given the differences in the children's emotional, motivational, and intellectual development, resisting an impulse to snatch a toy tends to be significantly harder for the younger children.

In some cases, five-year-olds may have an urge to snatch a toy from a younger sibling and just haul off and do it, without giving the matter any thought. In others, they may have an urge to snatch it, think (perhaps only very briefly) about whether or not to do so, and decide to take it. Consider the first time a normal child, Tony, makes a decision about whether to snatch a toy from his younger sister. He has impulsively grabbed his sister's toys in the past, but this time he gives the matter some thought and makes a decision. Tony knows that his father is nearby; and, on the basis of some unpleasant experiences, he associates taking the toy with his sister's screaming and his father's scolding him. He decides not to snatch it and feels a little frustrated. Imagine that Tony's father saw that he was tempted to take the toy and was inconspicuously watching his son to see what he would do. When he saw Tony move away from his sister and pick up something else to play with, he praised him for his good behavior. The father wasn't simply trying to reinforce the good behavior; he believed that Tony really deserved some credit for it.

Suppose now that owing to Tony's being an indeterministic decision-maker and to his being tempted to take the toy, there was a significant chance at the time that he would decide to take it. In Ufive, he decides not to snatch the toy. But in another universe with the same past and laws of nature, Usix, he decides to grab it and immediately proceeds to do so—with predictable results. Does that entail that Tony has no moral responsibility at all in Ufive for deciding not to take the toy? Well, he's only a child; and if he can be morally responsible for anything, he can be so only in ways appropriate for young children (if moral responsibility is possible for young children). It doesn't seem at all outlandish to believe that Tony deserves, from a moral point of view, some blame in the universe in which he decides to snatch the toy and acts accordingly—but blame appropriate to his age and the nature of his offense, of course. If he does deserve some such blame in Usix, he has some moral responsibility for the decision. Similarly, the father's belief in Ufive that Tony deserves some moral credit for his good decision is far from outlandish. If he does deserve such credit, it's of a kind appropriate to his age and the nature of his action, and he has some moral responsibility for the decision.

Call the time at which Tony makes his decision t. The difference at t between Ufive and a universe like Usix with the same past and laws of nature in which Tony decides at t to snatch the toy is just a matter of luck. That should be taken into account when asking about Tony's moral responsibility in Ufive for deciding not to take the toy, as should his limited capacity for impulse control and his limited ability to reflect on and evaluate potential consequences of his behavior. But only a relatively modest degree of moral responsibility is at issue, and the question is whether the luck involved—or the luck together with other facts about the case—entails that the degree is zero. I doubt that the knowledge that all actual decision-making children are indeterministic decision-makers like Tony would lead us to believe that no children are morally responsible at all for any of their decisions. But let's see what you think about this by the end of this chapter.

The idea that our past decisions can contribute to our moral responsibility for our present decisions naturally leads us to wonder about the earliest decisions for which children are morally responsible. When we do wonder about that, we need to keep firmly in mind how young these children may be and how trivial their good and bad deeds may be by comparison with the full range of good and bad adult deeds. Tony's making the right or the wrong decision this time about the toy is not that big a deal, which is something for us to bear in mind when we try to make up our minds about whether Tony is morally responsible for his decision. If, when pondering whether indeterministic decision-makers can make a first decision for which they are morally responsible, a philosopher's mind is occupied by scenarios in which people make decisions about important moral matters, luck at the time of decision should strike that philosopher as at least seriously problematic, for reasons we have seen. But focusing on such scenarios will lead one astray when the question before us is about young children like Tony.

Galen Strawson, in a 2002 article, describes true or real moral responsibility as "*heaven-and-hell* responsibility," a kind of responsibility such that, if we have it, "it makes sense to propose that it could be just—without any qualification—to punish some of us with (possibly everlasting) torment in hell and reward others with (possibly everlasting) bliss in heaven" (p. 451). Obviously, no sane person would think that little Tony deserves torment in hell—eternal or otherwise—for his bad deeds or heavenly bliss for his good ones. But Tony might occasionally deserve some unpleasant words or some pleasant praise; and, to use Strawson's expression, "it makes sense to propose" that Tony has, for some of his decisions, a degree of moral responsibility that would contribute to the justification of these mild punishments and rewards—even if those decisions are made at times at which the past and the laws of nature leave open alternative decisions, owing to Tony's being an indeterministic decision-maker.

If no one can be morally responsible for anything, then, of course, Tony isn't morally responsible to any degree for deciding not to take the toy. But if people are morally responsible for some things, they have to develop from neonates into morally responsible agents; and Tony's decision not to take the toy is a reasonable candidate for an action for which he is morally responsible. If Tony is morally responsible to some degree for deciding not to take the toy, and if his being morally responsible for that depends on his having made that decision freely, then Tony *freely* decides not to take the toy.

Moral responsibility is very commonly and very plausibly regarded as a matter of degree. *If* young children and adults are morally responsible for some of what they do, it is plausible, on grounds of the sort I mentioned, that young children aren't nearly as morally responsible for any of their deeds as some adults are for some of their adult deeds. When we combine our recognition of that point with the observation that the good and bad deeds of young children are (with rare exceptions) relatively trivial in themselves, we should be struck by the implausibility of stringent standards for deserved moral praise and blame of young children—including standards that require the absence of present luck. And once even a very modest degree of moral responsibility is in the picture, we can start thinking about ways in which it is amplified over time—something I gestured at in chapter 4.

Many of our decisions are influenced by earlier decisions we have made. For example, reflection on a bad decision of ours sometimes greatly decreases the likelihood that we will make similar decisions in the future. Someone who decided to drive home while over the legal limit for alcohol and barely avoided disaster may decide never to do that again—and abide by that decision permanently. Unlike random number generators, many people are able to learn from their mistakes (which isn't to say that random number generators make mistakes), and people sometimes do, in fact, learn from their mistakes. This is one fact about us that may be put to use in developing a response to the problem of present luck.

The facts I just reported about actual decision-making are certainly about more than our internal conditions (as defined above); they are partly about the past. So the Snapshot View places these facts outside the sphere in which my proposed solution to the problem of present luck is to be found.

When some people reflect on stories like Joe's, as I told it in chapter 4—perhaps especially people who assume that the Snapshot View is true—they may ignore the sources of the probabilities (reflected on Joe's decision wheel) of Joe's deciding to rob the shop and his deciding to do the right thing instead. If they imagine that these probabilities come out of the blue (as they do for a few weeks in the modified tale about Joe that we looked at in this chapter), Joe may seem to be adrift in a wave of probabilities that were imposed on him, and, accordingly, he may seem not to have sufficient control over what he decides to be morally responsible for his decisions. But it's a mistake to assume that indeterministic decision-makers' probabilities of action are externally imposed or that such people are related to their present probabilities of action roughly as dice are related to present probabilities about how they will land if tossed. If it is known that Joe's pertinent probabilities shortly before noon are shaped by a long series of past intentional, uncompelled behavior of his, one may take a less dim view of Joe's prospects for being morally responsible for the decision he makes and his prospects for making it freely.

I used the analogy of an indeterministic roulette wheel for three purposes when discussing deep openness. First, it gives you a way of picturing deep openness at the time of decision-making. Second, it's a way of making the problem of present luck salient. Third, it gives you a feel for the idea that each of the different mental actions open to the person at the time—such things as deciding to rob a shop, continuing to think about what to do, and so on—comes with its own probability of being what happens next. If the options and probabilities are set by a random device, we have what I called the problem of present luck on steroids. But if, in significant part, the options and probabilities are shaped over time by the person's own uncompelled behavior, including reflection on his or her own past behavior, the prospects for free will and moral responsibility are brighter. Of course, it makes sense to wonder how the self-shaping process gets off the ground. I have had something to say about that too.

One potential disadvantage of the roulette wheel analogy is that it may give some readers the impression that decision-makers aren't actually making decisions—that, instead, something is just happening in a neural mechanism in their heads. I want to cancel that impression. Recall that, as I put it, the ball's landing in a certain slot *is* the person's performing the mental action designated by that slot. You can think of the landing as what happens at the neural level of things when a person with deep openness makes a decision.

3. Deep Openness and Free Will

Does deep openness make a positive contribution to free will, as fans of a Mixed conception of free will claim? Here's one avenue to explore. Suppose that Frankfurt-style stories (discussed in chapter 3) don't work—that they all have some fatal flaw or other. Then the Principle of Alternative Possibilities is back on the table. Here it is again:

PAP (for acting freely). A person did something, *x*, freely at a time only if, at that time, it was open to her or him to do something other than *x* instead.

Traditional compatibilists endorse this principle, as you know, and they believe that being able to do otherwise than one did is compatible with determinism (see chapter 3, section 4). Different compatibilists offer different ways of interpreting the ability to do otherwise according to which determinism doesn't prevent people from having this ability. And, as you saw in chapter 3, incompatibilists object either that what the compatibilists offer is not actually an ability to do otherwise or that an ability to do otherwise, on any compatibilist interpretation, falls short of the robust kind of ability we need in order to act freely. One thing the latter sort of ability depends on, incompatibilists contend, is that the person's universe isn't deterministic. If you agree with incompatibilists about this, then you should see deep openness as having at least one thing going for it when it comes to free will. The person with deep openness at a time has an indeterminism-dependent ability to do otherwise. So if acting freely depends on having an ability to do otherwise that can only be had in an inde-terministic universe, having deep openness satisfies one necessary condition for free action.

I asked whether deep openness makes a contribution to free will. If having an indeterminism-dependent ability to do otherwise is a necessary condition for acting freely, then the answer is yes. Why is that? Because having deep openness is sufficient for having such an ability. Deep openness has an apparent downside too; it raises the problem of present luck. Does the upside of deep open-ness outweigh the downside? Are things the other way around?

For present purposes, let's continue to assume that Frankfurt-style stories don't work. I've suggested that the downside of deep openness will look much worse than it actually is if we assume that the probabilities regarding what a person with deep openness will do next come out of the blue. If, instead, we assume that these prob-abilities are shaped, in significant part, over time by the person's past intentional, uncompelled behavior, things look different.

Let's make a brief return to childhood. Part of my reason for going on about little Tony is that if free will and moral responsibility are to be possible for human beings, there has to be some way of getting from *zero* to *some*. If children can get to *some*, then by the time a normal child reaches adulthood, the "past intentional, uncompelled behavior" that I mentioned will include many free actions and many actions for which he or she is morally responsible. And if one's present probabilities for what one will do next are, in significant part, the outgrowth of a lengthy series of past free actions and past actions for which one was morally responsible, including reflection on the consequences of previous decisions one made and efforts at self-control, the problem of present luck doesn't look so daunting.

Did I do something sneaky in the preceding paragraph? There I'm working my way toward an explanation of how the problem of present luck is surmountable, and I say that if children can get from *zero* to *some* on a free will and moral responsibility scale, then by the time normal children reach adulthood (in normal circumstances), they will have performed many free actions and many actions for which they were morally responsible. Doesn't the problem of present luck arise for each of these free and morally responsible actions, assuming deep openness at the time? Yes, it does. But part of the point is that if we can see how a child can get over the hump for free action and moral responsibility, we are on our way to seeing how to respond to the problem of present luck whenever it arises. In the normal course of events, these children with deep openness will take on greater responsibility for how their wheels are configured as they mature. Their initial moral responsibility can blossom into full-blown adult moral responsibility. Some luck will be involved in any decision they make with deep openness. But not so much luck (normally, at least) that the decision is unfree and one for which they lack moral responsibility. Or so, at least, I'm suggesting.

You may recall my suggestion, in chapter 4's whirlwind tour of deep openness, that inhabitants of an indeterministic universe may be capable of configuring their decision wheels over time in such a way that they have no chance at all of making very bad decisions against their better judgment. This is something to which people may reasonably aspire. Of course, they would not be thinking in terms of decision wheels (unless they read this book). Instead, they'd be thinking in terms of good old-fashioned self-improvement or character development. In any case, decisions made with deep openness can contribute to self-improvement and to the development of one's character.

In this section, we've been assuming for the sake of argument that Frankfurt-style stories don't work, thereby putting the Principle of Alternative Possibilities back on the table. As we saw, if that principle is true, and if, more specifically, having an indeterminism-dependent ability to do otherwise is a necessary condition for acting freely, then deep openness makes a positive contribution to free will by satisfying a necessary condition for it. But what if some Frankfurt-style story does work—say, the story about Harry and Mary in chapter 3? If the idea works in one case, we can imagine that on *every* occasion when Mary makes a decision, there are only two ways things can go: either she decides on her own to do that thing, or she decides to do that very thing because Harry's manipulation issues in that decision. In that case, Mary is never able to decide otherwise than she does; and even so, assuming that the story works, she sometimes decides freely. We can even imagine that *whenever* Mary makes a decision, she makes it on her own (and therefore not because of Harry's manipulation). This may be extremely implausible, but that doesn't make it impossible. And a possibility is all that's needed here.

If this *global* Frankfurt-style story succeeds in doing what it is meant to do, can deep openness make a contribution to free will? Here, we need to be careful. What you as a decision-maker need for deep openness when you make your decision to have Wheaties for breakfast, as we have seen, is that more than one course of action is open to you, given everything as it actually is at the time—your mood, all your thoughts and feelings, your brain, your environment, and, indeed, the entire universe and its entire history. So you can see that deep openness entails indeterminism. And you can see that it entails something more than that too—namely, that you were able at the time to do something other than decide to have Wheaties for breakfast. If some Frankfurt-style story works, you don't need this *something more* in order to decide freely. But what about the first bit—indeterminism? Can indeterminism make a contribution to free will, even if free will doesn't depend on an ability to do otherwise?

It may be tempting to think that indeterminism can contribute to free will only by contributing to an ability to do otherwise. But, as I said, we need to be careful. Someone who believes that Frankfurt-style stories hit their mark may believe that something other than an ability to do otherwise is needed for free will and absent in any deterministic universe. What's needed, this person may say, is an ability of another kind—an ability to make a causal contribution to some of your decisions that isn't entailed by a true description of the laws of nature and the state of your universe at some time long before you were born. Call this an ability to be an *indeterministic originator* of some of your decisions.

Imagine that when Mary is on her death bed at the age of ninety-nine, Harry visits her and spills the beans. He informs Mary that every decision she ever made is one that he would have caused her to make if she hadn't indeterministically made it on her own. Harry describes a pair of chips he installed in Mary's brain long ago as part of a long-term experiment. One monitors her decision-making processes. And the other one is ready to cause Mary to decide on a particular option unless she indeterministically decides on that option on her own.

After some thought, Mary replies that although Harry definitely should not have treated her like a guinea pig, she's fine with how things turned out. Here's what Mary said:

> Well, I made all those decisions on my own. Those decisions are down to me, not to you. As far as my decisions go, it's as though you didn't do anything at all to me. After all, your tinkering had no effect on my decisions. Also, that I would make those decisions on my own wasn't already in the cards; it wasn't entailed by a complete statement of the laws of nature and a complete description of the universe long ago, as it would be if our universe were deterministic. So I'm confident that I'm responsible for my decisions and made them freely. If you had caused me to decide as I did, those decisions would not have been free. And, as I see it, those decisions would not have been free if they had been the inevitable consequences of the laws of nature and the way things were in the distant past. But that's not the way it was. You definitely should not

have screwed around with my brain, you jerk, but in the end
you had no effect on how my life went.

At this point, Mary decided to ask her nurse to escort Harry out of
her hospital room. Harry knew that this is what Mary would decide; but, once again, Mary made her decision on her own.

Mary's position is coherent. That is, it doesn't contradict itself.
She values what I called indeterministic initiation. And, in addition to valuing it, she regards it as a necessary condition for free
decision-making. Furthermore, she takes it to be a necessary condition for this even when decision-makers aren't able to do otherwise than make the decision they make, as in a Frankfurt-style
story. If there's a problem with this position, it's not that the position is self-contradictory.

If a compatibilist were to ask Mary why she believes that indeterministic initiation is necessary for free will, how might she
respond? To help put her auditor in her shoes, Mary might start
by talking about her values. She might report that the thought of
her actions as links in a long deterministic causal chain is deflating
and that the truth of determinism is inconsistent with her life's
being as important and meaningful as she hopes it is. The thought
that she is an indeterministic initiator of her decisions, however,
coheres with the importance and significance she hopes her life
has. Mary might observe that *independence* is among the things
that some people deeply value. Some people value independence,
in some measure, from other people and from institutions. Mary
values, as well, a measure of independence from the *past*. She
values a kind of independent agency that includes the power to
make a special kind of contribution to some of her actions and

to her world—contributions that are not themselves ultimately deterministically caused products of the state of the universe in the distant past. Mary values having a kind of causal bearing on her conduct that she can't have in any deterministic universe. She prizes being an indeterministic initiator of her decisions as an essential part of a life that she regards as most desirable for her. The kind of agency she hopes for, Mary might say, would render her decisions and actions personally more meaningful from the perspective of her own system of values than they would otherwise be.

Some people might value the kind of agency Mary values because they prize a kind of *credit* for their accomplishments that they regard as weightier than compatibilist credit. But Mary would report that although she respects this attitude, she doesn't share it. Her personal concern isn't with pluses and minuses in a cosmic ledger but with the exercises of agency to which these marks are assigned. It isn't credit that interests her, she would say, but independence. More fully, it's independence as manifested in rational decisions and other rational actions. Mary might acknowledge that she values compatibilist independence, but she would report that she values indeterministic independence more highly.

Mary is trying, she might say, to understand why some people might not share her preference for incompatibilist independence over a compatibilist counterpart. She might report that she is keeping an open mind and urge us to do the same. Mary hopes that we can understand why, other things being equal, she would deem her life more important or meaningful if she were to learn that determinism is false than if she were to learn that it is true.

To be sure, Mary may never know whether she has or lacks indeterministic independence, but that doesn't undermine her preferences. I hope that I will never know how my children's lives turned out (for then their lives would have been cut too short); but I place great value on their turning out well. There is nothing irrational in this. Nor must there be anything irrational in Mary's prizing her having a kind of agency that she can never know she has. This is another point I would expect Mary to make.

Having made it this far, Mary might acknowledge that she has not offered an *argument* for the proposition that free will depends on indeterminism. Instead, she's been telling her compatibilist auditor about her values and life hopes. At this point, she might simply say that she can't bring herself to believe that among all the wonderful things a deterministic universe may have to offer, one of them deserves to be called *free will*. Anything that doesn't include the indeterministic independence she values, Mary might say, simply doesn't count as free will in her book.

In the last several paragraphs, I've been trying to explain why someone who believes that some Frankfurt-style story shows that the Principle of Alternative Possibilities is false might also believe that free will depends on indeterminism. Notice that Mary's explanation of her incompatibilist position doesn't include any appeals to an ability to do otherwise. She explains what she takes to be important about a decision's not being deterministically caused without even mentioning an ability to do otherwise. I'm not saying that Mary's position should be *your* position. Instead, I've been trying to clarify why someone may believe that indeterminism can contribute to the freedom of a decision without contributing to an ability to do otherwise.

4. Recap

Given the length and complexity of this chapter, a brief recap will prove beneficial. The chapter has had three main goals. The first was further development of the problem of present luck posed by a Mixed conception of free will and the deep openness that that conception involves. As in chapter 4, we got some mileage out of the roulette wheel analogy.

The second goal was to sketch a potential solution to the problem of present luck. The potential solution we considered acknowledges the existence of present luck whenever a decision is made with deep openness and offers an explanation of why it is that the luck involved leaves room for free decision-making. The proposed solution has two parts. One part motivates the idea that present luck should not be seen as precluding the making of one's first free and morally responsible decision in childhood. The second part explains how one's moral responsibility for one's decisions can be amplified over time in people who have deep openness. And, of course, this more robust moral responsibility (like its less robust counterpart) depends on free will, given a popular view of the connection between free will and moral responsibility.

The third goal was to describe a view of how deep openness may make a positive contribution to free will. This was done from two different perspectives. The first perspective is that of someone who believes that Frankfurt-style stories don't falsify the Principle of Alternative Possibilities and that alternatives that are compatible with determinism aren't the robust alternatives that we need for free will. From that perspective, deep openness makes a contribution to free will by being sufficient for the satisfaction of what is claimed to be a necessary condition for free will—namely, having robust alternative possibilities. The second perspective is that of someone who believes that some Frankfurt-style stories succeed in doing what they are meant to do. From this perspective, free will doesn't depend on an ability to do otherwise. And if that's right, a part of deep openness isn't needed for free will. But that leaves something that's included in deep openness and is claimed to be necessary for free will—namely, indeterminism in decision-making. I had Mary explain why someone may maintain that this indeterminism contributes to free will even in people who, owing to the monkey business in a Frankfurt-style story, weren't able to do otherwise than decide to eat Wheaties for breakfast, or decide to rob a store, or whatever.

6 | SOME SOURCES OF SKEPTICISM

You can make it easy to argue that something—anything at all, including free will—doesn't exist by setting the bar for its existence extremely high. Here's an example. Sam claims that there have never been any great baseball players. The existence of great baseball players, he says, is an illusion. When we ask him to explain, he replies that a great baseball player would need to have a batting average of .450 or better for at least twenty consecutive seasons, pitch at least a dozen perfect games, and hit a minimum of two thousand home runs; and he correctly reports that no one has ever come anywhere close to this amazing performance. If that's what it takes to be a great baseball player, then no great baseball players have ever existed, and Sam has made his point. But, of course, normal baseball fans set the bar for greatness far lower, and we aren't at all embarrassed about doing so. Babe Ruth and Willie Mays were great baseball players, and so were a host of others. Sam's requirements for greatness are ridiculously high.

1. Bar Setting

Do some people set the bar for free will ridiculously high? In my opinion, yes. Here's an example from a 2008 article by neuroscientist Read Montague in *Current Biology*:

> Free will is the idea that we make choices and have thoughts independent of anything remotely resembling a physical process. Free will is the close cousin to the idea of the soul—the concept that "you," your thoughts and feelings, derive from an entity that is separate and distinct from the physical mechanisms that make up your body. From this perspective, your choices are not caused by physical events, but instead emerge wholly formed from somewhere indescribable and outside the purview of physical descriptions. This implies that free will cannot have evolved by natural selection, as that would place it directly in a stream of causally connected events. (p. 584)

The thrust of this passage, obviously, is that free will is an utterly magical notion.

In another example of extravagant bar-setting that features magic, biologist Anthony Cashmore, in a 2010 article, claims that "if we no longer entertain the luxury of a belief in the 'magic of the soul,' then there is little else to offer in support of the concept of free will" (p. 4499). He adds, "In the absence of any molecular model accommodating the concept of free will, I have to conclude that the dualism of Descartes is alive and well. That is, just like

Descartes, we still believe (much as we pretend otherwise) that there is a magic component to human behavior" (p. 4503).

In his 2011 book, *Who's in Charge? Free Will and the Science of the Brain*, neuroscientist Michael Gazzaniga says that free will involves a ghostly or nonphysical element and "some secret stuff that is YOU" (p. 108). Obviously, Gazzaniga, like Montague and Cashmore, isn't reporting a scientific discovery about what *free will* means. All three scientists are telling us what the expression *free will* means to them. Given what Gazzaniga means by *free will*, it's no surprise that, in his view, "free will is a miscast concept, based on social and psychological beliefs . . . that have not been borne out and/or are at odds with modern scientific knowledge about the nature of our universe."

The overwhelming majority of philosophers currently writing about free will don't see free will as magical, supernatural, or unnatural. They would reject as outlandish the descriptions of free will offered by Montague, Cashmore, and Gazzaniga. Should they and this trio of scientists just agree to disagree? Or can some headway be made?

A philosopher and a biologist, Ann and Azim, walk into a bar. Before long, they find themselves talking about free will. And within just a few minutes, they come to see that they mean very different things by *free will*. Azim claims that Ann is using the expression in a specialized way that is out of touch with ordinary usage, and Ann replies that it's Azim who's out of touch. Is there a way to support or undermine these claims?

Here's an idea. There's an interesting body of work in social psychology and experimental philosophy on what nonspecialists mean by *free will*. It uses survey studies, and many thousands of people have now been surveyed. If Ann and Azim were to look into this work, they would discover that it supports the idea that the bold claims about the meaning of *free will* that I have quoted from Montague, Cashmore, and Gazzaniga are accepted by only a minority of people. For example, even if lots of people believe in souls, there's considerable evidence that many of them don't regard free will as something that depends on the existence of souls.

In response to claims like Montague's, I conducted some simple survey studies of my own (first reported in a 2012 article of mine, "Another Scientific Threat to Free Will?"). In the study in which the absence of anything nonphysical—immaterial souls, for example—was made most salient, I polled a group of ninety Florida State University undergraduates taking a basic philosophy course that didn't deal with free will. The students read the following text: "We're interested in how you understand free will. Please read the following sentences and answer the questions by circling your answer." About half then read Story 1 below before they read Story 2; the others read the stories in the opposite order. The students were instructed not to change their answer about the story they read first after reading the other story. The questions were these: "Did John have free will when he made his decision?" and "Is this your first philosophy class after high school?" Participants' options for answers were *yes* and *no*.

Story 1: In 2019, scientists finally prove that everything in the universe is physical and that what we refer to as "minds" are actually brains at work. They also show exactly where decisions and intentions are found in the brain and how they are caused. Our decisions are brain processes, and our intentions are brain states. Also, our decisions and intentions are caused by other brain processes.

In 2009, John Jones saw a 20-dollar bill fall from the pocket of the person walking in front of him. He considered returning it to the person, who did not notice the bill fall; but he decided to keep it. Of course, given what scientists later discovered, John's decision was a brain process and it was caused by other brain processes.

Story 2: In 2019, scientists who work for a secret military organization finally develop a fool-proof compliance drug. The drug is used to make people decide to do various things. Whenever they give a person the drug and then suggest a course of action, that person is irresistibly caused to decide to take that course of action. They make their suggestions through a tiny computer chip that they implant in a person's brain.

These chemists gave the compliance drug to John Jones, a very honest man. When John saw a 20-dollar bill fall from the pocket of the person walking in front of him, they suggested keeping it. John considered returning it to the person, who did not notice the bill fall; but, of course, he decided to keep it. After all, the combination of the compliance drug and the suggestion forced John to decide to keep it.

The results are telling. Almost three quarters (73%) of the respondents said that John had free will when he made his decision in Story 1, and only about one fifth (21%) said this about John in Story 2. The strong negative response to Story 2 indicates that the great majority of respondents don't take a free-will-no-matter-what perspective. And Story 1, in which *physicalism* (the idea that everything that exists is physical) is very salient, yields a strong *free will* response. That story leaves no place in the universe for nonphysical entities to be at work. These findings clash with the claim that ordinary usage of the expression *free will* treats free will as a supernatural power that depends on the existence of immaterial souls. Although I certainly don't see my polls as foolproof, they definitely provide better evidence about ordinary usage of *free will* than does, for example, a randomly selected neuroscientist's opinion about what that expression means.

A 2018 follow-up study was part of a much larger study by Andrew Vonasch, Roy Baumeister, and me ("Ordinary People Think Free Will Is a Lack of Constraint, Not the Presence of a Soul"). Participants read one of four randomly assigned probes. The two probes that are most pertinent for present purposes are reproduced below (386 participants completed the questionnaire and passed our comprehension check).

Story A: Imagine that scientists finally discover that there are no souls. So, for example, they discover that you don't have a soul, that your friends and neighbors don't have souls, and so on.

Story B: Imagine that scientists finally discover that there are no souls. So, for example, they discover that you don't have a soul, that your friends and neighbors don't have souls, and so on. Like everyone else, John doesn't have a soul. One day, he sees a twenty-dollar bill fall out of the pocket of the person in front of him. He picks it up and keeps it for himself.

Participants responded to three statements about each story on a scale from 1 to 7, where 1 is "strongly disagree" and 7 is "strongly agree." The following statements accompanied Story A: People have free will in this situation; People can make conscious decisions in this situation; People are morally responsible for their actions in this situation. The statements accompanying Story B were specifically about John: John has free will in this situation; John can make conscious decisions in this situation; John is morally responsible for his actions in this situation.

Counting answers of 1, 2, and 3 as expressing disagreement and answers of 5, 6, and 7 as expressing agreement, we calculated the percentage of people who agreed with the statements and the percentage who disagreed. The results (rounded to the nearest whole number) are reported in table 6.1.

Here again we have evidence that a substantial majority of nonspecialists don't believe that free will depends on souls. And the same goes for moral responsibility.

A comment on the sociology of philosophy is appropriate here. A survey of 931 philosophers on thirty philosophical topics yielded some data on free will. When the "accept" and

Table 6.1

	Story A		Story B	
	Agree	Disagree	Agree	Disagree
Free Will	73%	18%	90%	4%
Conscious Decisions	75%	19%	91%	3%
Morally Responsible	70%	17%	86%	9%

"lean toward" responses are combined, the responses to the free will query break down as follows: "compatibilism 59.1%, libertarianism 13.7%, no free will 12.2%, other 14.9%" (Bourget and Chalmers 2014, p. 476). (Reminder: libertarianism is the combination of incompatibilism and belief in free will.) Now, believing that compatibilism is true doesn't commit one to believing in free will. Someone might think that although free will is compatible with determinism, there's good reason to believe free will doesn't exist. But, in practice, compatibilists believe in free will. When we add in the other pro-free-will position, libertarianism, we get a pro-free-will response of about 73 percent. (In principle, some people who fall under "other" may also believe in free will. For example, it's possible to be agnostic about the dispute between compatibilists and incompatibilists, not lean in either direction, and believe in free will.) So, then, do most of the philosophers surveyed believe in a divine being or beings? No. Here's the breakdown: atheism 72.8 percent, theism 14.6 percent, other 12.6 percent (p. 476). And, of course, it's a rare atheist philosopher who believes in immaterial souls. So we have evidence that the majority of philosophers—like the majority of nonspecialists—don't agree with those scientists who claim that free will depends on souls. (I should add that libertarianism was positively correlated with each of the following: theism, non-physicalism, and non-naturalism. People who are attracted to either libertarianism or theism tend to be attracted to the other as well.)

This strikes me as a reasonable place to say something about why I conceive of free will as I do. Often, an attempt to get a good grip on a concept benefits from an effort to fit it into a web of associated concepts. In ordinary thought, free will is closely associated with moral responsibility. When *moral responsibility* replaces *free will* in questions about stories of the kind I've been discussing, the percentage figures tend to be very similar, as they are in table 6.1. Free will and moral responsibility are closely connected in philosophical work as well. A common claim in the philosophical literature on these topics is that a being who never has free will isn't morally responsible for anything (though there are dissenters, of course).

Thinking about free will in connection with moral responsibility can bring some people down to Earth. It's noteworthy in this connection that although Gazzaniga rejects free will as magical and contrary to science, he takes a very different view of moral responsibility and accountability. "There is no scientific reason not to hold people accountable and responsible," he writes (p. 106). Someone might say that it's a good idea to hold people responsible even if they aren't, in fact, responsible, but Gazzaniga isn't advocating that idea. Evidently, he sets a much lower bar for responsibility than for free will—one that doesn't require anything supernatural. But, of course, he has no neuroscientific grounds for setting the bar for free will where he does. Nothing that comes from neuroscience prevents him from lowering his bar for free will to bring it into line with his naturalistic bar for moral responsibility. If he were to do that, he might start saying that there is no scientific reason to believe that free will is an illusion!

I conceive of free will as I do partly because I regard having free will—that is, an ability to act freely—as a necessary condition for being a morally responsible person, and I see no good reason to think that moral responsibility depends on the supernatural. Of course, this opens another can of worms. After all, there are people who contend that morality needs a supernatural foundation—that morality has God as its source. Pursuing that issue would take me far afield.

I've heard it said that my written work on free will and neuroscience dodges the idea that anyone who knows what *free will* means knows that free decisions need to issue from supernatural processes. The reason that survey-style experimental philosophy figures prominently in my discussion of this issue is that I believe this is the best approach to take to make headway with, for example, biologists who insist that free will is supernatural and aren't likely to be impressed by philosophical arguments about this. They know that their work in biology doesn't give them any special insight into what the expression *free will* means, and data on how nonspecialists use that expression are relevant to its meaning. Do I believe that survey-style experimental philosophy can settle such questions as whether free will is compatible with determinism and whether free will exists? No. But it is useful in the present context.

2. Two Skeptical Philosophical Arguments

Let's turn now to some familiar philosophical arguments for the nonexistence of free will. Sam Harris writes: "Free will is actually more than an illusion (or less), in that it cannot be made conceptually coherent. Either our wills are determined by prior causes and we are not responsible for them, or they are the product of chance and we are not responsible for them." This quotation is from Harris's *Free Will* (p. 5). That book's thesis is that free will doesn't exist. The book has sold very well, but I have to say that I often don't know exactly what Harris means by various claims he makes. In fact, this is part of the reason I haven't written a word about his book until now. In any case, there's a familiar old argument that bears some resemblance to the passage I quoted from Harris's book. I call it the *No Free Will Either Way Argument*. It goes like this:

No Free Will Either Way Argument

1. Either determinism is true or determinism is false.
2. If determinism is true, we don't have free will (because, in that case, everything is determined by prior causes).
3. If determinism is false, we don't have free will (because, in that case, we act randomly).
4. So we don't have free will.

You know by now that no compatibilist will accept this argument's second premise. Compatibilists maintain that decisions and other actions that are deterministically caused can be free. I don't see anything in Harris's book that's at all likely to convert a compatibilist to incompatibilism.

For readers who are not compatibilists, we should have a look at the argument's third premise. The mere falsity of determinism doesn't entail anything especially interesting about our behavior. Consider Useven, an indeterministic universe. On several of its planets, there are human beings a lot like us. There is some indeterminism in human brains there, but it has no significant bearing at all on human behavior. This is possible.

If there's a culprit in the ballpark of the third premise, it's the existence of indeterministic processes of the sort some incompatibilist believers in free will call for—for example, indeterministic processes associated with the problem of present luck. Recall the story about Joe and the gun in chapter 4. When Joe decided to rob the shop, did he decide randomly? Was his decision "the product of chance," to use Harris's phrase?

Joe's decision to rob the shop was made for reasons—reasons he had for committing the robbery. In that respect, his decision wasn't random. It didn't come out of the blue. Was his decision "the product of chance"? I'm not sure what that is supposed to mean. Chance itself doesn't produce anything. To be sure, given that Joe made his decision with deep openness, it was open to him to do something else at the time; there was a chance that he would do something else then. But I have already made a case for the claim that this is compatible with his making his decision freely. At one point Harris writes, "If certain of my behaviors are truly the result of chance, they should be surprising *even to me*" (p. 28). However, as we have seen, the options had by people who make decisions with deep openness are constrained by their psychological condition at the time—their beliefs, desires, hopes, and so on. Deep openness doesn't necessarily leave open options that are surprising in the way Harris imagines.

Here's something else from Harris's book:

Consider what it would take to actually have free will. You would need to be aware of all the factors that determine your thoughts and actions, and you would need to have complete control over those factors. But there is a paradox here that vitiates the very notion of freedom—for what would influence the influences? More influences? (pp. 13–14)

Here, Harris is setting the bar for free will preposterously high. Why on Earth should it be thought that you need to be aware of *everything* that influences your thoughts and actions in order to have free will? And why would you need to have complete control over these influences? However, I didn't quote this passage to give you yet another example of exaggerated bar setting. I quoted it because it expresses a theme in Harris's book that can be shaped up into another argument against the existence of free will. The theme is that free will requires an impossible regress of free actions. And the argument may be formulated as follows:

Impossible Regress Argument

1. In order for an action of yours to be a free action, it must express your values, desires, or the like.
2. If your values, desires, or the like aren't products of earlier free actions of yours, then actions expressing them aren't free.
3. So if you were to perform any free actions at all, they would always depend on earlier free actions of yours that produce the values, desires, or the like that you express. That is, if you were ever to do anything freely, then every free action that you perform would depend on at least one earlier free action that you performed.
4. But what step 3 describes is impossible for real human beings. You'd have to have an infinite past in order for each free action of yours to be preceded by another free action of yours.
5. So free actions are impossible for real human beings.

What's your reaction to this argument? You might have predicted mine. A conception of free will that is meant to apply to human beings should acknowledge the fact that neonates don't act freely. If people are to act freely, they must develop from beings who haven't ever acted freely into beings who sometimes do act freely. This contradicts the argument's second premise. So what is more plausible—that the second premise is true or that people can make the transition I just mentioned? In chapter 5, I offered some support for the idea that the transition can indeed be made.

We'll examine more philosophical arguments for the nonexistence of free will in the next chapter. It's time to leave Harris behind and wrap this chapter up.

Here, we examined two kinds of route to the conclusion that free will doesn't exist. The first featured the device of setting the bar for free will absurdly high, and the second highlighted a pair of familiar philosophical arguments.

In my discussion of the bar-setting maneuver, I appealed to the results of some work in experimental philosophy. Neuroscientists, for example, know that the simple fact that they are neuroscientists doesn't give them any special insight into what the expression *free will* means. (Some neuroscientists may believe that philosophers don't have any special insight into its meaning either, and they may offer as evidence the fact that philosophers disagree with each other on this topic.) Nora, a neuroscientist friend of mine, can be led to entertain the thought that her understanding of that expression may be an artifact of her own personal upbringing and to consider the hypothesis that she is out of touch with ordinary usage of *free will*. In experiments with human participants, scientists definitely prefer to have a sample size larger than one person; and, like any scientist, Nora can see that if the way she goes about determining what *free will* means is simply to consult her own feeling or intuition about the meaning, then—to the extent to which it is important to avoid being mistaken about the meaning of *free will*—she should seek a better method. (The simple, navel-gazing method isn't recommended for philosophers either, of course.) That's why I appealed to results in experimental philosophy. Those results should discourage extravagant bar-setting for free will.

My responses to the two philosophical arguments that I considered—the No Free Will Either Way Argument and the Impossible Regress Argument—were pretty brief. That's because the foundation for those replies had already been laid in previous chapters. Of course, it's possible that other arguments may succeed where those arguments failed. And, as I said, we'll be examining more skeptical arguments.

7 | MORE SKEPTICAL ARGUMENTS

In chapter 2, I introduced you to some technical terminology. A brief reminder is in order now, before we look into some further skeptical arguments. By the way, I'm confident that you'll remember the first two terms and their meaning. But you might not remember the third term; I haven't used it much. Because it's defined in terms of the first two, I'll start with them. So here you go. *Compatibilism* is the thesis that free will can exist in a deterministic universe. (Compatibilists have what I called a Straight conception of free will.) *Incompatibilism* is the thesis that compatibilism is false. (Many incompatibilists have a Mixed conception of free will.) *Libertarianism* is incompatibilism plus the thesis that free will exists. (As you'll recall, libertarianism about free will is to be distinguished from political libertarianism.)

Libertarian positions on free will divide into three general kinds, as you'll see. In this chapter, we'll explore arguments for the nonexistence of free will that have the following structure.

A. First, it is argued that a particular libertarian view is right about what it takes to have free will. Let's call what it takes X.
B. Then it is argued that X doesn't exist.
C. The conclusion is drawn that free will doesn't exist.

Exploring arguments with this structure will enable me to explain libertarian ideas more fully than I have done so far while also extending the discussion of skepticism about free will that we embarked on in chapter 6.

1. Three Libertarian Theories

When Martin Luther was accused of heresy and asked to recant, he reportedly said, "Here I stand, I can do no other." Many scholars doubt that he actually said this. But that is neither here nor there for present purposes. Suppose Luther couldn't have done otherwise than refuse to take back various things he said. And suppose that the causes of his refusal that were closest in time to that refusal—its *proximate* causes—deterministically caused his refusing to recant. Must a libertarian say that Luther's refusal wasn't free? Not necessarily. Some libertarians make a distinction between *directly* and *indirectly* free actions. A deterministically caused action may be said to count as indirectly free if it inherits freedom from earlier free actions that aren't deterministically caused—that is, from directly free actions the person performed. So, for example, if a lengthy series of past undetermined actions that Luther performed led him to have a character of such a kind that recanting wasn't possible for him, his refusing to recant may be indirectly free. To make things more manageable than they would otherwise be, I'll limit the ensuing discussion of free will to actions that are supposed to be directly free.

Generally speaking, libertarian theories about free will come in three different varieties: *event-causal*, *agent-causal*, and *noncausal*. According to typical event-causal libertarian theories, the proximate causes of directly free actions indeterministically cause them. This is a consequence of the typical event-causal libertarian ideas that directly free actions have proximate causes and that if a person (directly) freely does something at a time *t*, then in some possible universe in which the entire past up to *t* and the laws of nature are the same, he or she doesn't perform that action at *t*. It should be noted that the proximate causes of actions, including such mental actions as decisions, are internal to the beings who are acting—to the *agents*, as philosophers like to say. Even a driver's sudden decision to hit his or her brakes in an emergency situation isn't proximately caused by events in the external world. Perception of whatever the source of the emergency happens to be—for example, a dog darting into traffic—is causally involved. And how drivers decide to react to what they see depends on, among other things, their driving skills and habits, whether or not they are aware of what is happening directly behind them, and their preferences. A hypothetical driver who likes driving over dogs and relishes opportunities to do that would probably react very differently from a normal person. And drivers who, benefiting from their rearview mirror, see that a sudden stop would cause a serious collision may behave differently from drivers who are unaware of the car just behind them. In light of the general point about the proximate causation of actions, typical event-causal libertarianism encompasses a commitment to *agent-internal* indeterminism—indeterministic processes within the person.

Whereas the laws of nature that apply to deterministic causation are exceptionless, those that apply most directly to indeterministic causation are instead probabilistic. So if the occurrence of x (at time $t1$) indeterministically causes the occurrence of y (at $t2$), then a complete description of the universe at (and before) $t1$ together with a complete statement of the laws of nature doesn't entail that y occurs at $t2$. (You'll recall the discussion of entailment in chapter 2.) There was at most a high probability that the occurrence of x at $t1$ would cause the occurrence of y at $t2$. As you'll recall, events like *deciding* to give a hitchhiker a ride—as distinct from the physical actions involved in actually giving the person a ride—are deemed mental *actions*. Suppose that Harry's decision to give a hitchhiker a ride is indeterministically caused by, among other things, his thinking that he should do this. Because the causation is indeterministic, he might not have decided at the time to offer him a ride given exactly the same internal and external conditions. In this way, some libertarians seek to secure the possibility of doing otherwise that they require for free action. This is familiar territory to you by now. (And you will have noticed that we've been ignoring Frankfurt-style stories in this section. I decided to do that to simplify exposition.)

What libertarians require for free action that determinism precludes isn't merely that we sometimes have open to us more than one future that is compatible with the combination of the past and the laws of nature, but also that, on some occasions, which possible future becomes actual is in some sense and to some degree up to us. Event-causal libertarians require something that entails that people themselves are indeterministic in some suitable way—that some relevant things that happen under the skin are indeterministically caused by other such things. The focus is on mental events (or their neural correlates), as opposed, for example, to indeterministically caused muscle spasms—and, more specifically, on mental events that have a significant bearing on action (or, again, the neural correlates of these events).

Quantum mechanics, according to some interpretations, is indeterministic. But indeterminism at that level doesn't ensure that any human brains sometimes operate indeterministically in ways appropriate for free action. One possibility is that any indeterminism in the human brain itself is simply irrelevant to the production of actions. A scientific discovery that this possibility is an actuality would show that we don't have free will according to some familiar libertarian conceptions of it.

Agent-causal libertarianism is the next theory on our agenda. Agents are beings who act. You and I are agents. Agent-causal libertarianism features *agent causation*—that is, causation of an effect by an agent. Think of causation as a relation between cause and effect. In ordinary event causation—for example, a falling tree knocking over a fence—both cause and effect are events. The cause includes the tree's crashing into the fence, and the fence's collapsing is an effect. These events are connected by the relation *causation*. In agent causation, an agent is connected by the relation causation to an effect—and connected in a way that isn't reducible to a connection among events. Whereas most agent-causal libertarians prefer their agent causation straight, some mix it with causation by events in a theory about how free actions are caused.

I said that the way in which agent-causes are supposed to be connected to what they cause isn't reducible to a connection among events. What did I mean by that? We say things like *A rock broke the window*. For most of us, this is shorthand for something like the following: a rock's hitting the window—an event—caused the window to break. In light of this we can say that rock causation (that is, causation by rocks) is reducible to causation by events involving rocks. Agent causation isn't like that. It isn't reducible to causation by things—like events—that aren't agents.

The most straightforward reason offered for building agent causation into a theory of free will has to do with an alleged shortcoming of event-causal libertarianism that is brought out nicely by the problem of present luck, discussed at some length in chapter 5. That problem casts doubt on whether people of the kind event-causal libertarians count as free have enough control over what they do to act freely. Agent causation is supposed to solve this problem.

How is it supposed to solve the problem? Agent-causal libertarians have two different ways to go in response to this question. One is to explain what it is supposed to be about causation by an agent (as opposed to causation by events) that bestows on a person what might be termed *freedom-level control* over what he or she causes. The other is simply to build it into the notion of agent causation—by stipulation—that it includes freedom-level control and then challenge others to disprove the theory.

Let's start with the first route. It has been suggested that by combining indeterministic causation by events (where the term *events* is understood broadly to include mental states like beliefs and desires) with agent causation, a philosopher identifies a greater power for beings who act than what is provided by indeterministic causation by events alone. But even if this is true (and I'm not saying it is), there is no guarantee that the combined or greater power is up to the task. Here's an analogy. I may try to lift a weight using the power of only one arm and fail. I may try again, this time also using the power of my other arm; and I may fail again, the combined powers not being up to the task. If the weight is a ton, the combined powers aren't enough to give me even a ghost of a chance of lifting it. The combination of agent causation with indeterministic causation by states and events may be similarly inadequate when it comes to acting freely.

As you'll recall, most agent-causationists prefer their agent causation straight; they don't mix it with causation by events. So suppose someone claims that the agent-causal power is beefier—greater—than any power that can be found in causation by events. A problem that is very similar to the one we just considered immediately arises. The power's being beefier doesn't necessarily mean that it's up to the task.

Does agent causation—alone or in combination with causation by events—provide a solution to the problem of present luck? Return to the beefed-up version of the story about Joe and the gun in chapter 5 and add just one detail: Joe has the power of agent causation. In the present version of the story, as in the counterpart story in chapter 5, Joe does his best to resist his urge to rob the shop. He goes all out to beat down the temptation to commit the robbery he is contemplating. He focuses on the possible unwanted consequences of the evil deed, on the kind of person he wants to be, and so on. But, in the end, he decides to rob the shop. In another possible universe that's exactly the same right up to that point, Joe's efforts pay off; he decides instead not to rob it. His efforts of self-control—like everything else up to the moment of decision—were exactly the same in both universes, but those efforts failed in one and succeeded in the other.

I'll repeat, from chapter 5, my description of one way of thinking about the problem of present luck as it arises in the story I told there:

> If there is nothing about Joe's abilities, capacities, state of mind, moral character, reasoning, efforts at self-control, and the like in either universe that accounts for the difference in what he decides, then the difference seems to be just a matter of luck. And given that neither universe differs from the other in any respect at all before he makes his decision, there is no difference at all in Joe in these two universes to account for the difference in his decisions.

This statement applies just as well to the present story in which Joe agent-causes his decision. In one universe he agent-causes his decision to rob the store, and in another universe in which everything is the same right up to the time of decision, he agent-causes a decision not to rob the store.

It's difficult to see how agent causation, understood simply as a causal relation between an agent and an event, even makes a dent in the problem of present luck. Perhaps that is why some philosophers have wanted to build it into the very notion of agent causation that agent-causing an event is sufficient for freely causing it. We'll return to this issue later.

The stage is now set for one of the skeptical arguments about free will that we'll be examining in this chapter. But before we get to that argument I want to do two things. First, I want to make a technical point about the literature on agent causation. Second, I want to explain the third kind of libertarianism to be discussed here—noncausal libertarianism.

What events are agent-caused, according to agent-causal libertarians? I said that Joe agent-causes his decision to rob the shop, and some agent causationists would say this too. But others would say that he agent-causes his intention to rob the shop and that his deciding to rob it should be understood as his agent-causing that intention. This difference doesn't matter for my purposes in this book. But I would have felt guilty if I had left readers with the false impression that all agent-causationists agree on what is and isn't agent-caused.

Now for the third kind of libertarianism. A straightforward noncausal libertarian view asserts that only uncaused actions can be free. A source of motivation for this position—specifically as a competitor to the other brands of libertarianism—can be framed in terms of luck. The claim is that these competing positions make it too much a matter of luck what people decide for it to be up to them what they decide and for them to decide freely. A philosopher can argue for this claim as follows:

1. Event-causal libertarian views make it too much a matter of luck what people decide for them to decide freely.
2. Agent-causal libertarian views have the same problem.
3. So both event-causal libertarianism and agent-causal libertarianism are undermined by the problem of present luck.

Of course, this isn't yet an argument for noncausal libertarianism. Even if this argument were successful and these two brands of libertarianism face insurmountable problems, noncausal libertarianism might face insurmountable problems too.

2. More Arguments for Skepticism About Free Will

I said that we'd be exploring arguments for the nonexistence of free will that have the following structure.

A. First, it is argued that a particular libertarian view is right about what it takes to have free will. Let's call what it takes X.
B. Then it is argued that X doesn't exist.
C. The conclusion is drawn that free will doesn't exist.

We're in a position to do that now.

Here's a sketch of the first argument to be considered. I call it the *agent-causation-based skeptical argument*—or *ASA*, for short.

ASA (the agent-causation-based skeptical argument)

1. Free will depends on agent causation.
2. Agent causation doesn't exist.
3. So free will doesn't exist.

To mount a convincing argument of this kind, you need convincing arguments for both premises. When a premise is obviously true, there's no need to argue for it. But these premises aren't obvious.

One way to argue for the first premise begins with an argument for incompatibilism. The next step is to argue that kinds of libertarianism that don't appeal to agent causation don't manage to provide sufficient conditions for free will. Then one can argue that if there's anything that can provide what's missing, it's agent causation. People who proceed in this way may offer the arguments for incompatibilism that we've already discussed—the argument based on the story of Diana and Ernie (*ZAF* in chapter 2) and the Consequence Argument (discussed in chapter 3)—or they may try to produce superior arguments for incompatibilism. In arguing against event-causal libertarianism, they may try to get some mileage out of the problem of present luck (discussed in chapter 5). And to make a case for the need for agent causation, they may try to explain how—if agent causation exists—it would solve this problem.

What about *ASA*'s second premise, the claim that agent causation doesn't exist? Different arguments have been offered for that premise. Some philosophers argue that only events can be causes. It has also been argued that to do the theoretical work it's supposed to do, agent causation can't be constrained by laws of nature and that there's no evidence of the existence of a kind of causation that isn't constrained by laws of nature. Of course, believers in agent causation resist these arguments.

In my own writing on agent causation, I've resisted the claim that free will depends on it (which amounts to resisting *ASA*'s first premise). As I see things, even if there is such a thing as agent causation, it doesn't solve the problem of present luck; and I believe that the problem can be solved by event-causal libertarians in the way sketched in chapter 5. If I'm on the right track, the biggest problem with *ASA* is the absence of a convincing argument that free will depends on agent causation.

I mentioned that an agent-causationist can stipulate that agent causation incorporates freedom-level control and challenge others to disprove this. How should we respond to this tactic? Well, suppose that an *event-causal* libertarian were to stipulate that causation in the right way by events incorporates freedom-level control and challenge agent-causationists to disprove this. One likely response from agent-causationists is an argument that features the problem of present luck. The argument can be used as a basis for rejecting what is stipulated. But if, as I have suggested, agent-causal libertarianism is faced with the same problem, the same kind of argument can be used as a basis for rejecting the stipulation about agent causation.

It's time to have a look at an argument for the nonexistence of free will that's based on the idea that free actions must be uncaused.

USA (the uncaused-action-based argument for the nonexistence of free will)

1. Free actions must be uncaused.
2. No actions are uncaused.
3. So there are no free actions and free will doesn't exist.

As we saw, *USA*'s first premise can be partially motivated by the claim that event-causal and agent-causal libertarian positions make it too much a matter of luck what people decide for it to be up to them what they decide and for them to decide freely. We'll take a look at this premise shortly.

What about *USA*'s second premise? I believe it's true. I can't give you a complete explanation here of why I believe that. A complete explanation would involve rebutting various attempts to explain how actions can be uncaused. But I can point you in my direction.

Sometimes we think we're acting for one reason when we're actually acting for another reason. Often, our mistakes in this sphere are self-serving. Here's an example. Jane's aunt Joan is very ill. She has terminal pancreatic cancer and isn't able to do anything for herself. Jane has been taking care of her for several months. Today, Jane decided to give Joan a lethal dose of pain medication. She believes that she made this decision only to put Joan out of her misery. But, in fact, she made it in order to relieve herself of the burden of caring for her aunt.

This story makes perfect sense. What can we infer from it, assuming that the story is true? In Jane's opinion, her decision was motivated by a desire to benefit her aunt, whereas, in fact, it was motivated by a desire to benefit herself. Jane's decision makes sense in light of either desire. But, it seems, the truth about why she made the decision she made depends on which of the two desires actually played a suitable causal role in producing the decision.

Consider a version of Jane's story in which you're not explicitly told why Jane made her decision. This version is set in a distant future in which neuroscientists are able to selectively disconnect motives from the decision-making process. They can, for example, sever any potential connection between Jane's desire to put Joan out of her misery and a decision to give Joan a fatal dose while not interfering in any way with her desire to be free of the burden of caring for her aunt. If that's what the scientists do, it's hard to resist the conclusion that which of the two causal pathways is open tells us what motivated Jane's decision. (We're assuming that no third pathway is relevant.)

It's hard to deny that actions have causes. And if actions do have causes, we should ask whether *USA*'s first premise—the claim that free actions must be uncaused—should be believed. If you think that there can be causation only in deterministic universes and you are an incompatibilist, you'll be attracted by the idea that free actions are uncaused. But you know better than that: indeterministic causation of actions is possible. We noticed that people can try to find support for the claim that free actions are uncaused in the idea that event-causal and agent-causal libertarian positions lack the theoretical resources to solve the problem of present luck. But, as we saw, this underestimates their resources (see chapter 5). As you know, I favor a solution from an event-causal libertarian perspective. So here is my bottom line on *USA*: Even if all actions are caused, the argument fails, because it's false that free actions must be uncaused.

3. Another Argument

In this chapter, we examined a pair of arguments for the nonexistence of free will. One of them, *ASA*, was based on the idea that free will depends on agent causation; and the other one, *USA*, was based on the idea that free actions must be uncaused. This chapter's primary aim was to explain libertarian ideas more fully than previous chapters did. At this point, you should have a pretty good understanding of the three kinds of libertarianism: event-causal, agent-causal, and noncausal.

You might have expected to see an examination of a third kind of argument as well—a skeptical argument based on the idea that free will depends on indeterministic causation by events and states, an event-causal libertarian thesis. Here is one such argument.

ESA (an indeterministic event-causation-based skeptical argument)

1. Free will depends on indeterministic proximate causation by events.
2. Actions caused in this way are too lucky to be free.
3. So free will doesn't exist.

We didn't examine *ESA* in this chapter because I responded to it, in effect, in chapter 5, where I offered a solution to the problem of present luck on behalf of event-causal libertarians.

8 | FREE WILL AND NEUROSCIENCE

Experiments performed by neuroscientist Benjamin Libet in the 1980s are often cited as proof that free will is an illusion. (By the way, *Libet* rhymes with the sound a cartoon frog makes, *Ribbit*.) Some neuroscientists have followed in Libet's footsteps, sometimes using electroencephalography (EEG), as he did, and sometimes using functional magnetic resonance imaging (fMRI), depth electrodes, or subdural grid electrodes. (I'll fill you in on these different technologies later.) In my 2009 book, *Effective Intentions*, I argued that the neuroscientific work discussed there, including Libet's, falls well short of justifying the claim that free will is an illusion. My focus was on the data and on whether the data supported certain empirical claims that have been combined with theoretical claims about free will to yield the conclusion that free will doesn't exist. There are some interesting new data now. After I provide essential background, we'll explore the bearing of some experiments published after 2009 on the question of whether we have convincing neuroscientific evidence for the nonexistence of free will.

1. Background

Based on the results of various experiments of his, Libet makes the following claims:

> The brain "decides" to initiate or, at least, prepare to initiate [certain actions] before there is any reportable subjective awareness that such a decision has taken place. (1985, p. 536)

> If the "act now" process is initiated unconsciously, then conscious free will is not doing it. (2001, p. 62)

> Our overall findings do suggest some fundamental characteristics of the simpler acts that may be applicable to all consciously intended acts and even to responsibility and free will. (1985, p. 563)

Associated with these claims is the following skeptical argument about free will. Let's call it the *decision-focused skeptical argument*, or *DSA* for short.

DSA (the decision-focused skeptical argument)

1. In Libet-style experiments, all the decisions to act on which data are gathered are made unconsciously.
2. So probably all decisions to act are made unconsciously.
3. No unconsciously made decision to act is freely made.
4. So probably no decisions to act are freely made.

In *Effective Intentions*, I devoted a lot of space to showing that the first premise isn't justified by the data and some space to explaining why the generalization in the second premise isn't warranted. We'll return to the former matter shortly, after I provide some background. The latter matter is addressed in section 4.

You will have noticed that *DSA* is about decisions in particular rather than actions in general. Even if all decisions are unfree, that leaves it open that some actions of other kinds are free. We won't pursue this line of thought here. Decisions (or choices) lie at the heart of the philosophical literature on free will, and the discovery that there are no free decisions would be an extremely serious blow to free will. So we'll stay focused on decisions in this chapter.

Recall that decisions to do things, as we're conceiving of them, are momentary actions of forming intentions to do those things. For example, to decide to flex your right wrist now is to perform an action of forming an intention to flex it now. Libet understands decisions in the same way. And he studies *proximal* decisions (or intentions or urges) in particular. Proximal decisions (in the simplest cases) are decisions to do something *right now*. Similarly, proximal intentions and urges (in the simplest cases) are intentions and urges to do something right now. There are also *distal* decisions—decisions we make to do something later. The decision I made recently to join some friends for lunch tomorrow is a case in point.

In the experiments to be described in this section, participants are asked to report on when they had certain conscious experiences—variously described as experiences of an urge, intention, or decision to do what they did. After they act, they make their reports. The measure of consciousness in these experiments is the participants' reports on this matter. We can call the kind of consciousness at issue *report-level consciousness*.

The expression *W time* or *time W* is sometimes used in the literature on Libet's work as a label for the time at which participants are first conscious or aware of their proximal intention (or decision or urge) to flex a wrist and sometimes for the *reported* time of first awareness or consciousness of this. The two times may be different; the reports might not be accurate. And Libet himself thought that although the average reported time is about 200 milliseconds (one-fifth of a second) before muscle motion begins, the actual average time is about 150 milliseconds before the beginning of muscle motion. Here I use *time W* as a label for the actual time of first awareness. I'll also follow the common convention in scientific writing of using *ms* as shorthand for *milliseconds*. That will save some ink.

Libet's main innovation was a method for timing conscious experiences that can then be correlated with measurable brain events. He was particularly interested in experiences of proximal urges, intentions, or decisions. Participants in his experiments that receive the most attention are instructed to flex a wrist whenever they feel like it and then report a bit later on when they first became conscious of their decision, intention, or urge to flex.

During the experiment, participants watch a Libet clock. It's fast: a spot revolves around the clock face in about two and a half seconds. The participants, sitting in chairs, report their belief about where the spot was on the clock when they first became aware of their proximal decision, intention, or urge to flex. A bit after they flex, the clock stops moving and it's time to make their report. A straightforward reporting method is simply to say where they think the revolving spot was when they first felt the urge to flex. During my stint as a subject in a Libet-style experiment at the National Institutes of Health years ago, I made my reports by moving a cursor to mark that place on a computerized clock.

Libet takes readings of electrical conductivity from the scalp, using EEG technology. Brain activity involves measurable electricity—more in different places, depending on what parts of the brain are most active. EEG technology uses electrodes on the scalp (or electrode caps these days) to detect this activity. In order to produce readable EEGs, Libet's participants flex at least forty times during each session. Readings are also taken from the wrist so that Libet can tell when muscle motion begins during wrist flexes. At the beginning of muscle motion, there's a burst of muscle activity—a *muscle burst*.

When participants in Libet's experiments are regularly reminded not to plan their wrist flexes and when they don't say afterward that they did some such planning, an average ramping up of EEG activity precedes the average reported time of the conscious experience (200 ms before muscle motion begins; *−200 ms*, for short) by about a third of a second. The initial ramping starts a bit more than half a second (550 ms, to be precise) before muscle motion begins. Libet claims that decisions about when to flex were made at the earlier of these two times: −550 ms, as measured backward from the beginning of muscle motion. And he concludes that these decisions are made unconsciously. His reasoning is simple. If you make a proximal decision to flex at −550 and you don't become conscious of that decision for another 350 ms or so, then you weren't conscious of your decision when you made it—you made your decision unconsciously, as this conclusion is often put.

Of course, one thing this reasoning depends on is the claim that the decision was made at or around −550 ms. We'll examine that claim pretty soon.

When thinking about Libet's reasoning, the following timeline might come in handy.

```
        −550 ms            −200 ms                    0 ms
time:--------x--------------------x----------------------------x-------------->
        RP onset      reported time W    muscle begins to move
```

Keep it in mind as you read on.

The initial ramping that I mentioned is the beginning of a readiness potential (RP), which may be understood as "a progressive increase in brain activity prior to intentional actions, normally measured using EEG, and thought to arise from frontal brain areas that prepare actions" (Haggard and coauthors 2015, p. 325). We'll discuss the significance of RPs shortly.

Chun Siong Soon and coauthors, commenting on Libet's work, write: "Because brain activity in the SMA [supplementary motor area] consistently preceded the conscious decision, it has been argued that the brain had already unconsciously made a decision to move even before the subject became aware of it" (2008, p. 543). To gather additional evidence about the proposition at issue, they use fMRI (functional magnetic resonance imaging) in a study of participants instructed to do the following "when they felt the urge to do so": "decide between one of two buttons, operated by the left and right index fingers, and press it immediately" (p. 543). This technique measures changes in blood flow in the brain to see what parts of the brain were most active in the past few seconds.

Nothing hinges on which button is selected; the participants have nothing to gain or lose. In this respect, the choice of a button is similar to the choice of a moment to begin flexing; nothing hinges on which moment is selected.

Soon and colleagues find that, using readings from two brain regions (one in the frontopolar cortex and the other in the parietal cortex), they are able to "predict" with about 60 percent accuracy which button participants will press several seconds in advance of the button press. (The prediction referred to isn't real-time prediction. That is, the experimenters aren't predicting button presses in advance of the participants' presses. After the fact, they look for correlations between readings of brain activity and button presses.)

In another experiment, Soon and coauthors ask participants to decide between the two buttons at a predetermined point in time. The participants are supposed to make a decision about which button to press when shown a cue and then act on the decision later, when presented with a *respond* cue. Again, nothing hinges on which decision participants make. Soon and colleagues report that one interpretation of this experiment's findings is that "frontopolar cortex was the first cortical stage at which the actual decision was made, whereas precuneus was involved in storage of the decision until it reached awareness" (p. 545).

In an experiment reported in a 2011 article, Itzhak Fried, Roy Mukamel, and Gabriel Kreiman record directly from the brain, using depth electrodes. Although depth electrodes have been used since the 1950s, the technology is more sophisticated now. People with severe epilepsy sometimes opt for a procedure that requires removing part of the skull. Electrodes are placed on the surface of the brain—and sometimes a bit beneath the surface. The purpose is to identify places where seizures are generated so surgery can be performed on bits of the brain responsible for the seizures. Electrical recordings directly from the brain are much more informative than EEG readings, since the electricity measured by EEG has to travel through the thick bone of the skull.

If patients wish, they can participate in various experiments while the electrodes are in place, including Libet-style experiments. Fried and coauthors report that "a population of SMA neurons is sufficient to predict in single trials the impending decision to move with accuracy greater than 80% already 700 ms prior to subjects' awareness" (p. 548) of their "urge" (p. 558) to press the key. By "700 ms prior to subjects' awareness," Fried and his colleagues mean 700 ms prior to the awareness time that participants later *report*: they recognize that the reports might not be accurate. And, unlike Libet, they occasionally seem to treat decisions to press keys as things that are, by definition, conscious. Possibly, in their thinking about their findings, they identify the participants' decisions with conscious urges. If that's how they use the word *decision*, their claim here is that on the basis of activity in the SMA they can predict with greater than 80 percent accuracy what time a participant will report to be the time at which he or she was first aware of an urge to press 700 ms prior to the reported time. But someone who uses the word *decision* differently may describe the same result as a greater than 80 percent accuracy rate in detecting decisions 700 ms before people become aware of a decision they already made. These two different ways of describing the result obviously are very different. The former description doesn't include an assertion about when the decision was made.

I just now implicitly distinguished between urges and decisions. That distinction is important when the topic is free will. Although lots of people believe that we make many of our decisions freely, who would say that we freely produce many of our urges? Our urges normally come to us unbidden, as an urge to scratch my itchy ankle did a moment ago. And it certainly seems that we can feel an urge to do something and decide not to do it. Think of dieters with an urge to eat a second helping of dessert or ex-smokers with an urge for a cigarette. They can have an urge to eat or smoke without deciding to do that; and, indeed, they can decide *not* to do it. Decisions—and not urges—lie at the heart of philosophical discussions of free will. The distinction is one to keep in mind.

There are grounds for doubt about the accuracy of the reported awareness times in the experiments we've been looking at. I discussed such grounds in chapter 6 of *Effective Intentions* and I won't do so again here. Instead, we'll focus on two questions. The first question is this: When are the pertinent decisions made in these experiments (if the participants make decisions)? The second is a question about the point of no return in action-producing processes. I'll introduce it later, in connection with a skeptical argument that's related to *DSA*.

2. When Do Participants Make Their Decisions?

In the preceding section, I described experiments by three different groups of scientists that are often claimed to show that free will doesn't exist. In this section and the next two, I'll explain why these experiments don't have this consequence.

In *Effective Intentions*, drawing on data of various kinds, I argued that Libet's participants don't make decisions as early as 550 ms before the beginning of muscle motion (−550 ms). Drawing on the same data, I also suggested there that early stages of the readiness potential in his main experiment (a type II RP, which begins at −550 ms) may be associated with a variety of things that aren't decisions or intentions: "urges to (prepare to) flex soon, brain events suitable for being relatively proximal causal contributors to such urges, motor preparation, and motor imagery, including imagery associated with imagining flexing very soon" (p. 56). Call this group of things *the early group*. As I pointed out, "If RP onset in cases of 'spontaneous' flexing indicates the emergence of a potential cause of a proximal intention to flex, the proximal intention itself may emerge at some point between RP onset and time W, *at* time W, or *after* time W: at time W the agent may be aware only of something—a proximal urge to flex, for example—that has not yet issued in a proximal intention" (p. 57). (Reminder: time W is the first time at which participants are aware of the mental event they report on.) This point bears on *DSA*'s first premise, the assertion that in Libet-style experiments, all the decisions to act on which data are gathered are made unconsciously. If proximal decisions to flex—momentary actions of forming proximal intentions to flex—aren't made before W, Libet's argument for the claim that they are made unconsciously crumbles.

Also relevant in this connection is evidence about how long it takes for a proximal decision or proximal intention to generate relevant muscle motion. Does it take around 550 ms, as Libet's interpretation of his results implies? I discussed this issue in *Effective Intentions*, where I offered a data-based argument for a negative answer. There's additional evidence about this now. We'll look at one piece of it here.

In *Effective Intentions*, I suggested that some of the participants in Libet's experiments may treat the conscious urge to flex as what may be called a *decide-signal*—a signal calling for them consciously to decide right then whether to flex right away or to wait a while. Judy Trevena and Jeff Miller conducted a pair of interesting decide-signal experiments, reporting the results in an article published in 2010. For present purposes, their most important finding concerns muscle activity, measured using electromyography (EMG). Trevena and Miller report that EMG "seemed to start about 150 ms after the [decide-signal] tone" in relevant trials (p. 452). If a proximal decision or intention to tap a key followed the tone, then, obviously, the time from the onset of that decision or intention to muscle motion is even shorter. This casts serious doubt on the claim that, on average, proximal decisions or intentions to flex are made or acquired about 550 ms prior to muscle motion in Libet's experiments. Why? Because Trevena and Miller's finding indicates that the time from proximal intention acquisition to muscle motion is much shorter than 550 ms.

Given what we've seen so far in this section, how plausible is it that Soon and coauthors found decisions 7 to 10 seconds in advance of a button press? Partly because the encoding accuracy was only 60 percent, it's rash to conclude that a decision was actually made at this early time (7 to 10 seconds before participants were conscious of a decision). (Even if the encoding accuracy were much higher, one might reasonably wonder whether what is being detected are decisions or, instead, potential causes of subsequent decisions.) It is considerably less rash to infer that brain activity at this time made it a bit more probable that, for example, the participant would select the button on the left than the button on the right. The brain activity may indicate that the participant is, at that point, slightly more inclined to press the former button the next time he or she presses. Rather than already having decided to press a particular button next time, the person may have a slight unconscious bias toward pressing that button.

What about Fried and colleagues? Did they find early decisions? Their findings are compatible with their having detected at 700 ms before reported W time an item of one of the kinds mentioned in what I called *the early group*: urges to (prepare to) press a key soon, brain events suitable for being relatively proximal causal contributors to such urges, motor preparation, and motor imagery. If participants made proximal decisions to press a key, the findings are compatible with their having made those decisions as late as the decision time identified by Trevena and Miller.

3. When Do Participants Reach the Point of No Return?

Someone who is persuaded that, in the experiments we've discussing, decisions aren't made at −550 ms or earlier may believe that, even so, the *point of no return* for the action-generating processes is hit at one or another of the early times identified above and that this is bad news for free will. (The point of no return for a process is a point such that, other things being equal, once the process has reached it, the process will proceed to completion.) This belief suggests another argument for skepticism about free will. I'll call it *PSA*, where *P* stands for *point of no return*.

PSA (the point-of-no-return-focused skeptical argument)

1. In Libet-style experiments, the point of no return for processes that issue in overt actions is reached well before the corresponding decisions are made.
2. So this is probably true in all cases in which decisions to act are made.
3. If the point of no return for an action-generating process is reached well before the corresponding decision is made, then the decision is not freely made.
4. So probably no decisions to act are freely made.

Someone who endorses this argument's third premise may contend that if the point of no return for an action is hit well before the corresponding decision is made, the point of no return for the *decision* is also hit at this early time. And this contention may be paired with the further claim that, in order for a decision to be free, there can be no time prior to the decision's being made at which the point of no return for the making of it has been reached. (This alleged necessary condition for a decision's being free should call deep openness to mind.) Not everyone will accept these claims, of course; and not everyone will accept *PSA*'s third premise. (For example, in deterministic universes, the point of no return for processes is hit very early! And compatibilists don't see that as an obstacle to free will.) But, for our purposes here, the third premise doesn't need to be challenged. Our concern is *PSA*'s first premise.

In a comment on the possibility of *vetoing* an urge, intention, or decision, Libet makes the following observation: "In the absence of the muscle's electrical signal when being activated, there was no trigger to initiate the computer's recording of any RP that may have preceded the veto" (2004, p. 141). Given this fact about the design of Libet's main experiment, his data don't allow us to look for a point of no return. Suppose we wanted to use Libet's data to test the hypothesis that the point of no return for muscle motion is hit somewhere between 550 (when the type II RP starts ramping up) and 250 ms before muscle motion starts. What we would like to do is to look at the data to see whether we ever get readings that look like type II RPs during that span of time but aren't followed by muscle motion. Libet's experimental design doesn't allow us to do that. In the main experiment, we get readings only when there is muscle motion.

In *Effective Intentions*, I reported that if I had a neuroscience lab, I would conduct a stop-signal experiment of a certain kind to get evidence about the point of no return in Libet-style scenarios. An experiment of this kind has since been conducted, and it is much more elegant than the one I sketched back then.

The experiment, reported in a 2016 article by Matthias Schultze-Kraft and coauthors, takes place in three stages. In all three stages, there is a floor-mounted button, and a circle is presented on a computer monitor. After the circle turns green, participants wait for about two seconds. When they have finished waiting, they may press the button whenever they wish. They earn points if they press while the light is still green and lose points if they press after the light turns red. The red light is a stop signal.

In stage 1 of the experiment, the stop signals are issued at random times, and the participants are informed of this. Movement times are not predicted. EEG data from this stage are used to "train a classifier to predict upcoming movements in the next two stages" (Schultze-Kraft and coauthors 2016, p. 1080).

Stage 2 differs from stage 1 in that movement predictions are made in real time, using a brain-computer interface (BCI). The BCI uses electrical signals from the brain to predict when the person will press. Participants aren't informed of this before the experiment. The aim is to issue stop signals in time to interrupt the participants' movements.

After participants complete stage 2, they are told that the computer had been predicting what they would do and that they should try to move unpredictably. The participants are now ready for stage 3, which is just like stage 2 except that they now have the information I just mentioned.

For our purposes, the most interesting finding is the following one: "Despite the stereotypical shape of the RP and its early onset at around 1,000 ms before EMG activity, several aspects of our data suggest that subjects were able to cancel an upcoming movement until a point of no return that was reached around 200 ms before movement onset" (Schultze-Kraft and coauthors 2016, p. 1083). If this is when the point of no return for movement onset (that is, muscle motion) is reached, *PSA*'s first premise is false and the argument crumbles. Reminder: The first premise is the claim that in Libet-style experiments, the point of no return for processes that issue in overt actions is reached well before the corresponding decisions are made (where the decisions are said to be made anywhere from 550 ms to several seconds before muscle motion).

4. The Generalizing Maneuver

DSA and *PSA* share a certain strategy. Both arguments generalize from an alleged finding about *some* decisions to a claim about *all* decisions. In *DSA*, the alleged finding is that all the decisions on which data are gathered in Libet-style experiments are made unconsciously, and the generalization is that probably all decisions are made unconsciously. In *PSA* the alleged finding is that in Libet-style experiments the point of no return for processes that issue in overt actions is reached well before the corresponding decisions are made, and the generalization is that this is probably true in all cases of decision-making. I have been arguing that these alleged findings are illusions. But even if they weren't illusions, would we be entitled to infer that what is true of these particular decisions—made in specific laboratory settings—is probably true of all (or even most) decisions?

Some brief remarks on inductive reasoning are in order now. Cathy points out to Zeke that although he used to have twenty male cousins, he now has only ten. Ten of his male cousins died before reaching the age of fifty, and the ten living ones are, like Zeke, younger than fifty. Cathy says, "I hate to say this, Zeke. But your ten dead male cousins died before the age of fifty; so probably you and all of your remaining male cousins will also die before the age of fifty." At first, Zeke is worried, but then he gives the matter some thought. Of the ten dead cousins, five died during their participation in such extreme sports as free climbing, base jumping, and bull riding, and the other five were bank robbers who robbed one bank too many—they were all killed in the same attempted robbery. The remaining cousins, in contrast, lead safe, peaceful lives, as does Zeke. Given this difference between the two groups of cousins—the dead ones and the living ones—Cathy's inference in unacceptable. Her generalization is unwarranted.

A brief description of my own experience as a participant in a Libet-style experiment will also prove useful as background. I had just three things to do: watch a Libet clock with a view to keeping track of when I first became aware of something like a proximal urge, decision, or intention to flex; flex whenever I felt like it (many times over the course of the experiment); and report, after each flex, where I believed the hand was on the clock at the moment of first awareness. (As I mentioned, I reported this belief by moving a cursor to a point on the Libet clock.) Because I didn't experience any proximal urges, decisions, or intentions to flex, I hit on the strategy of saying *now!* silently to myself just before beginning to flex. This is the mental event that I tried to keep track of with the assistance of the clock. I thought of the *now!* as shorthand for the imperative *flex now!*—something that may be interpreted as an expression of a proximal decision to flex.

Why did I say *now!* exactly when I did? On any given trial, I had before me a string of equally good moments for a *now!*-saying, and I arbitrarily picked one of the moments. (I'm not saying that every moment was equally good. I wanted to avoid lengthening my participation in the experiment unnecessarily.) But what led me to pick the moment I picked? Frankly, I don't know. Should this worry me? I don't see why. If my brain uses unconscious mechanisms to break ties in trivial cases of arbitrary picking, that's fine with me. I can't think of a better way to do it.

In Libet-style experiments, participants are instructed to be spontaneous—that is, not to think about when to flex, which button to press, or the like. The instructions, if followed, keep consciousness out of the part of the decision-producing process that's at work shortly before the decision is made. (Consciousness may be causally involved earlier in the process: for example, participants' conscious understanding of the instructions has a claim to being causally relevant to their performance, and a participant may consciously make a plan for completing the experiment, as I did.) The main role for consciousness in these experiments is linked to reporting: participants need a conscious event to report to the experimenter in the case of each particular action. In my case, as I mentioned, that event was a conscious, silent speech act.

So one difference between decisions made in Libet-style experiments (when participants are following the instructions) and some other decisions is that some other decisions are preceded by conscious reasoning specifically about what to do. The existence of this difference challenges the generalizing maneuver in *DSA* and *PSA*. From the assertion that, when participants are instructed *not* to think about when to flex, they make their decisions about flexing unconsciously it doesn't follow that, when people do consciously reason about what to do, they make their decisions unconsciously. Perhaps conscious reasoning about what to do increases the likelihood of conscious deciding—that is, of being conscious of what you decide at the very time you make your decision. Someone who wants to argue that, even when we consciously reason about what to do, we make our decisions unconsciously can't rely solely on what happens in situations in which there is no directly relevant conscious reasoning. And the same goes regarding when the point of no return is reached. Someone who wants to argue that it is reached long before any decision is made even though the person is consciously reasoning about what to do can't rely solely on what happens in situations in which there is no such reasoning.

Another difference also merits attention. As I pointed out, during my stint as a participant in a Libet-style experiment I arbitrarily picked moments to begin flexing. Arbitrary picking is featured in the Libet-style experiments I described in section 1—the experiments by Libet, by the Soon group, and by the Fried group. Participants are said to have decided when to flex a wrist, when to press a key, or which of two buttons to press. There was no reason to prefer a particular moment for beginning to flex a wrist or press a key over nearby moments and (in the experiment by Soon and coauthors) no reason to prefer one button over the other. In these experiments, participants select from options they are indifferent about. But in many cases of decision-making, we are far from indifferent about our main options, and many instances of deciding aren't instances of arbitrary picking. In typical cases, when we make decisions about matters that are very important to us, after carefully gathering evidence and painstakingly assessing the options, our leading options differ from one another in ways that matter to us, and we don't arbitrarily pick.

The primary upshot of the considerations sketched in this section is easy to see. Arbitrary pickings in Libet-style experiments differ in obvious ways from some of the decisions we make—decisions about matters that we aren't indifferent about and that we make after careful reasoning about what to do. And the differences are such that we can't legitimately make the generalizations featured in *DSA* and *PSA*. That is, we can't legitimately generalize from the assertion that all decisions on which data are gathered in Libet-style experiments are made unconsciously—or the assertion that the point of no return is hit early in these situations—to the conclusion that this is probably true in all cases of decision-making. That line of reasoning is too similar to Cathy's faulty reasoning about Zeke's cousins.

I close this section with a comment on a recent experiment comparing arbitrary picking with decisions made in a scenario in which it makes good sense to engage in conscious reasoning about what to do (Maoz and coauthors 2019). In this experiment, participants have the opportunity to influence which charities on a certain list receive donations. Sometimes they arbitrarily pick a charity, and sometimes they have a good reason to engage in conscious thinking about what to do before deciding (nonarbitrarily) which of two charities to support. The experimenters report that although they "found the expected RPs for arbitrary decisions, [RPs] were strikingly absent from deliberate ones" (p. 1). And, as they observe, this striking difference challenges the idea that we can safely generalize from findings about arbitrary picking to claims about thoughtful decisions. This reinforces the main moral of this section. The experimenters also suggest that "two different neural mechanisms may be involved in arbitrary and deliberate decisions" (p. 19). This is a topic for future neuroscientific work.

5. A Thought Experiment

Let's turn now from laboratory experiments to a thought experiment. Even top-notch scientists can trip themselves up when interpreting the results of Libet-style experiments. I'll illustrate this claim of mine with a brief discussion of a thought experiment by neuroscientist V. S. Ramachandran.

Ramachandran's thought experiment starts as follows: "I'm monitoring your EEG while you wiggle your finger. . . . I will see a readiness potential a second before you act. But suppose I display the signal on a screen in front of you so that you can *see* your free will. Every time you are about to wiggle your finger, supposedly using your own free will, the machine will tell you a second in advance!" (2004, p. 87).

Ramachandran asks what you would experience, and he offers an answer: "There are three logical possibilities. (1) You might experience a sudden loss of will, feeling that the machine is controlling you, that you are a mere puppet and that free will is just an illusion. . . . (2) You might think that it does not change your sense of free will one iota, preferring to believe that the machine has some sort of spooky paranormal precognition by which it is able to predict your movements accurately. (3) You might . . . deny the evidence of your eyes and maintain that your sensation of will preceded the machine's signal."

Unfortunately for him, Ramachandran overlooked a very logical possibility. If I were a participant in the experiment, I'd definitely want to test the machine's powers. I'd watch for the signal to appear on the screen and then see if I can keep from wiggling a finger. Libet's data, as we saw, definitely leave it open that I can do this. There is no good reason to believe that what I see on the screen signifies that I have hit the point of no return for an impending finger wiggling.

Consider the following two sentences:

1. Whenever you wiggle your finger, signal S appears a second before you wiggle it.
2. Whenever signal S appears, you wiggle your finger a second later.

These sentences say two very different things. This is easy to see, especially when you consider two parallel sentences.

3. Whenever you win a lottery prize, you acquired a ticket before you won—you bought it or found it or whatever.
4. Whenever you acquire a lottery ticket, you win a lottery prize.

Obviously, sentence 3 doesn't entail sentence 4. You can't win a lottery unless you first get a ticket, but that doesn't mean that every ticket is a winner. Similarly, maybe you can't wiggle your finger unless signal S first appears, but that doesn't mean that every time the signal appears, you'll wiggle your finger.

If you succeed in keeping your finger still after you see the signal, maybe the signal is a sign of the presence of a potential cause of an intention or decision to wiggle your finger soon. Even when that potential cause is present, you might decide not to wiggle your finger and you might behave accordingly. In that case, you won't see the machine as controlling you. You won't be tempted to believe the machine has paranormal predictive powers. And you won't deny the evidence of your eyes. In short, you won't do any of the three possible things Ramachandran mentioned. You'll do a fourth possible thing—one he didn't mention.

6. The Bottom Line

The primary purpose of this chapter was to explain why we shouldn't be persuaded by two neuroscientific arguments—*DSA* and *PSA*—for the nonexistence of free will while paying special attention to some relatively recent experiments. These experiments add to the body of evidence supporting the conclusion that both arguments fail. I don't want to leave you with the impression that, in my opinion, the problems with these skeptical arguments that we have focused on here are the only problems with them. For example, in *Effective Intentions*, I raised worries about the reliability of reported W times. In any case, the bottom line is that neuroscience has not closed the door on free will.

9 | WRAPPING THINGS UP

Well, we've covered a lot of ground. In this final chapter, I'll highlight some of the main landmarks and say a bit more about my own take on free will.

1. Some Landmarks

By now, I hope you have a good grip on the following things.

1. *A Straight perspective on free will and some of its pros and cons.* Did the argument based on the story about Diana (a goddess) and Ernie (her creation)—that is, *ZAF* in chapter 2—incline you to doubt that conditions that are actually sufficient for free will can be identified from a Straight perspective? And what did you think about *RZAF* as a rebuttal of *ZAF*? (The handy index makes these arguments easy to find.) Did the discussion of Frankfurt-style stories persuade you that the ability to decide (or do) otherwise than you did isn't required for having decided freely? And what about the Consequence Argument (in chapter 3)? Did it convince you that determinism (as

understood in this book) leaves no room for free will? Did my critique of the Consequence Argument work for you?

2. *A Mixed perspective on free will and some of its pros and cons.* Did you find deep openness attractive as a necessary condition for free will? Did you find deep openness disturbing? What is your take on the problem of present luck? And what do you think about the solution I proposed?

3. *Arguments for skepticism about free will and their weaknesses.* We examined six such arguments. Four were theoretical arguments and two were grounded in neuroscience. Of the four theoretical arguments, two (A and B below) are general in nature and two (C and D below) are based on very specific philosophical views about what is required for free will. Here's a list, along with my bare-bones formulations of the arguments.

A. The No Free Will Either Way Argument
1. Either determinism is true or determinism is false.
2. If determinism is true, we don't have free will (because, in that case, everything is determined by prior causes).
3. If determinism is false, we don't have free will (because, in that case, we act randomly).
4. So we don't have free will.

B. The Impossible Regress Argument
1. In order for an action of yours to be a free action, it must express your values, desires, or the like.
2. If your values, desires, or the like aren't products of earlier free actions of yours, then actions expressing them aren't free.

3. So if you were to perform any free actions at all, they would always depend on earlier free actions of yours that produce the values, desires, or the like that you express. That is, if you were ever to do anything freely, then every free action that you perform would depend on at least one earlier free action that you performed.

4. But what step 3 describes is impossible for real human beings. You'd have to have an infinite past in order for each free action of yours to be preceded by another free action of yours.

5. So free actions are impossible for real human beings.

C. *ASA* (the agent-causation-based skeptical argument)

1. Free will depends on agent causation.

2. Agent causation doesn't exist.

3. So free will doesn't exist.

D. *USA* (the uncaused-action-based argument for the nonexistence of free will)

1. Free actions must be uncaused.

2. No actions are uncaused.

3. So there are no free actions and free will doesn't exist.

E. *DSA* (the decision-focused skeptical argument)

1. In Libet-style experiments, all the decisions to act on which data are gathered are made unconsciously.

2. So probably all decisions to act are made unconsciously.

3. No unconsciously made decision to act is freely made.

4. So probably no decisions to act are freely made.

F. *PSA* (the point-of-no-return-focused skeptical argument)

1. In Libet-style experiments, the point of no return for processes that issue in overt actions is reached well before the corresponding decisions are made.

2. So this is probably true in all cases in which decisions to act are made.

3. If the point of no return for an action-generating process is reached well before the corresponding decision is made, then the decision is not freely made.

4. So probably no decisions to act are freely made.

Were you persuaded by any of these arguments? Were you persuaded by my rebuttals of them? The latter, I hope.

4. *The bar-setting maneuver in support of skepticism about free will and my reply.* This maneuver, as you'll recall, is to place the bar for free will at dizzying heights. My reply was designed to bring us back down to earth, partly by surveying nonspecialists about (in effect) what *free will* means. After reading the preceding chapters, where are *you* inclined to set the bar for free will?

2. My Take on Free Will

As I said in chapter 1, my own position on free will is distinctive. I can describe it in terms of the following four propositions:

1. Free will exists and it is accurately characterized in a Straight way.
2. Free will exists and it is accurately characterized in a Mixed way.
3. Either proposition 1 is true or proposition 2 is true.
4. Free will does not exist.

In these terms, my position is that proposition 3 is more credible than proposition 4.

A comment on proposition 2 is in order now. What I have called deep openness is featured in my description of a Mixed conception of free will. Here's something I said about deep openness in chapter 4:

> Today, I thought about what to have for lunch and I decided on a cheese and tomato sandwich with a pickle on the side. I made that decision at noon. If I had deep openness at noon, then if time could be rewound to just a moment before I made my decision and then played forward, in some of the "replays" I would decide on one of the other options I was considering.

My having deep openness at noon, as I characterized deep openness, depends on it being undetermined right up to noon what I decide. Proponents of a Mixed conception of free will claim that having deep openness, so understood, right up until noon is *required* for deciding freely at noon. But is this a deeper or more extensive openness than is actually needed by libertarians?

Imagine two different scenarios in two different universes. In Ueight, it's open what I will decide right up to noon and, on the basis of my reflection on my options, I decide at noon on a cheese and tomato sandwich with a pickle on the side. In Unine, on the basis of my reflection on my options, I also decide at noon on a cheese and tomato sandwich with a pickle on the side, but I hit the point of no return for that outcome ten milliseconds before noon; at that point, the decision-producing process goes deterministic. In Unine, I fall ten milliseconds short of having what I called deep openness regarding the decision I made at noon. But a libertarian doesn't need to regard that fact as rendering my decision unfree. It was undetermined what I would decide until ten milliseconds before noon. And if that fact about indeterminism is combined with such facts as that I am sane, unmanipulated, and unpressured and consciously make my reasonable decision on the basis of good information, some libertarians may be happy to count my decision as freely made. I have focused on deep openness in my discussion of libertarianism because it's a common focal point and because of its relative precision. According to a more flexible Mixed conception of free will, not only does deep openness do free-will-supporting work in the sphere of indeterminism, but so does the kind of openness we get when we're a bit more relaxed about timing—that is, about how close to the time of decision it is still open what the person will decide. I won't speculate on how much relaxation is permissible.

My position, as I said, is that proposition 3 is more credible than proposition 4. Proposition 3 amounts to the following assertion:

P. Either (1) free will exists and it is accurately characterized in a Straight way or (2) free will exists and it is accurately characterized in a Mixed way.

So my position is that P is more credible than proposition 4 ("Free will doesn't exist").

Why do I settle for this position? For a collection of reasons. And I need to emphasize the word *collection*. My claim is that the reasons I'm about to present *collectively*—rather than individually—explain why I take the position I do.

So here we go. I'll start at the beginning. First, I don't regard any of the arguments for incompatibilism as decisive. As I see it, those arguments (including *ZAF* and the Consequence Argument) leave compatibilism on the table. And because I keep compatibilism on the table, I can't flatly endorse proposition 2, which embraces incompatibilism. Second, many thoughtful people have a respectable conception of free will that can't be satisfied by any compatibilist position, and I don't know of anything that should convince them that they're wrong to conceive of free will as they do. So I'm not in a position sincerely to assert that compatibilism is true. Third, on grounds that I've discussed, I find the arguments for the thesis that free will doesn't exist unpersuasive.

My reasons don't end here. But I need to set up the next one before presenting it. One option is to be agnostic about free will. There are different ways to be agnostic about an issue. Some people are agnostic about the existence of God, for example, because they haven't given the matter much thought and don't feel that they're in a position to have an opinion about the matter one way or the other. And some agnostics about the existence of God have given the matter a great deal of thought and believe that, all things considered, the most reasonable thing for them to do is neither to believe that God exists nor to believe that God doesn't exist. As a definite, reflective standpoint on free will, agnosticism about free will is the position that, when all is said and done, the most reasonable stand to take is to sit firmly on the fence on the question of whether or not free will exists. A proponent of this sort of agnosticism doesn't believe that free will exists and doesn't believe that free will doesn't exist. But he or she doesn't end up in this position in the way someone who has thought very little about free will might. Instead, an agnostic of the kind I have in mind has thought long and hard about free will and has concluded that agnosticism about the existence of free will is the most reasonable way to go.

My position on free will differs from agnosticism of this kind. After all, I believe that proposition P (a pro-free-will claim) is more credible than proposition 4 ("Free will doesn't exist"). So why do I believe that?

Let's start with the first half of P. If free will is accurately characterized in a Straight way, then it's very hard to deny that free will exists. To see this, have a look at Proposal 1 (from chapter 1). It's a statement of sufficient conditions for deciding freely that is made from a Straight perspective on free will—a compatibilist perspective.

> Proposal 1. If sane, unmanipulated people consciously make a reasonable decision to do something on the basis of good information and no one is pressuring them, they freely decide to do that thing.

I have no doubt that the overwhelming majority of readers of this book would report that they have made many decisions that fit this description. And these reports would be largely correct. So *if* free will is accurately characterized in a Straight way, free will exists. We should be confident of that. Of course, that little word *if* needs to be kept in mind. That's why I italicized it.

How confident should we be that free will is accurately characterized in a Straight way—that is, in a compatibilist way? That's hard to say. Compatibilists tend to be very confident that this characterization is accurate, and incompatibilists tend to be just as confident that it isn't. In chapter 2, I explored what I take to be the two best lines of argument for incompatibilism (*ZAF* and the Consequence Argument), and I explained why a critic can reasonably remain unpersuaded by them. I hasten to add that I also don't know of any knock-down argument for the thesis that compatibilism is true. So I've long been undecided about whether compatibilism is true or false.

Imagine that I have to place a bet one way or the other on compatibilism. (You can make up your own story about why that might be.) Imagine that my only options are *Compatibilism is true* and *Compatibilism is false*. How would I bet? And why?

To make matters more concrete, let's have a look at a version of Proposal 1 that is explicitly compatibilist:

> Proposal 1*. Whether or not determinism is true, if sane, unmanipulated people consciously make a reasonable decision to do something on the basis of good information and no one is pressuring them, they freely decide to do that thing.

Let's imagine that I have to bet on whether this proposal is true or false. I'd bet that it's true. I've already reminded you of my negative assessment of what I take to be the strongest arguments against compatibilism. What can be said in favor of compatibilism and Proposal 1*?

As we saw in chapter 3, compatibilists can distinguish between forced and unforced actions, and they can make a reasonable case for the idea that unforced decisions that have the additional features identified in Proposal 1* are free decisions. You may re-call the discussion in chapter 3 of compulsive hand-washers and normal hand-washers in this connection. Compatibilists can also invite us to reflect on how we would respond to a discovery by physicists that our own universe is deterministic, something I commented on in chapter 2. Would we give up on the idea that we have free will and everything that depends on it? I mentioned accountability, justified gratitude, and warranted resentment as examples of things that seemingly depend on free will. Would a discovery in physics warrant such a radical change in our view of ourselves and others? Should such a discovery instead leave things in the domain of ordinary life pretty much as they are? Would many people who weren't already compatibilists come around to the view that free will exists but isn't quite what they thought it was? And would that be a reasonable thing for them to do?

My own tentative, speculative thoughts about how these questions should be answered tip the scales in favor of compatibilism for me—that is, in the imaginary scenario in which I have to bet on whether compatibilism is true or false. (Because in real life I don't have to bet on this, I stay on the fence.) And, as I explained, if compatibilism is true, free will exists: many of our decisions satisfy the conditions set out in Proposal 1. So if I were to rank the following two propositions in terms of credibility, I would give 1 a higher ranking than 4.

1. Free will exists and it is accurately characterized in a Straight way.
4. Free will doesn't exist.

And if 1 gets a higher credibility rating than 4, so does 3 (which, as you'll recall, amounts to the assertion, P, that either (1) free will exists and it is accurately characterized in a Straight way or (2) free will exists and it is accurately characterized in a Mixed way). Why? Because 3 is a safer or more modest claim than 1. If 1 is true, so is 3. But 3 also has another way of being true—a way that doesn't depend on 1 being true. That's what makes 3 safer or less demanding than 1. Proposition 3 is safer than proposition 1 in just the way that my statement that my friend Tarik is thirty-eight or thirty-nine is safer than my statement that he's thirty-nine. (I know what year he was born in, but I don't remember the month.)

I also have a pragmatic reason for taking the position I do on free will. Seasoned compatibilists and incompatibilists are very firmly entrenched in their positions on this issue. In my opinion, my time would not be well spent trying to persuade members of either group to switch sides, and I myself haven't been persuaded that I should join either side anyway. But what I might be able to do is to construct for compatibilists a better compatibilist theory of free will than its compatibilist competitors and to construct for incompatibilist believers in free will—that is, for libertarians— a libertarian theory of free will that is superior to its libertarian competitors. Remaining neutral on whether compatibilism is true or false enables me to devote my time and effort to this theory-building project and to producing arguments designed to show that what I'm offering is, indeed, superior to rival theories in the same camp. For readers interested in this (sometimes technical) project, I recommend my *Free Will and Luck*, *Aspects of Agency*, and *Manipulated Agents*.

I've given you, in a nutshell, my reasons for taking the position I do on free will, and I've said quite a bit in this chapter about proposition 1, which concerns a Straight conception of free will. But what's my position on proposition 2—that free will exists and is accurately characterized in a Mixed way?

We've explored what I regard as a respectable Mixed conception of free will. That conception, as you know, is associated with the following proposal:

> Proposal 2. If sane, unmanipulated people consciously make a reasonable decision to do something on the basis of good information, no one is pressuring them, and they were able to make an alternative reasonable decision, in a sense of *able* that requires deep openness, they freely decide to do that thing.

Here, deep openness is mixed into Proposal 1, resulting in a proposal that is attractive to many libertarians. And, as I explained, a libertarian can be at least a bit more relaxed about the timing component of deep openness and endorse a more flexible version of Proposal 2. I'll call the type of openness to which such a version would appeal *deep-ish openness*. Deep-ish openness includes deep openness but also includes openness that ends a bit earlier, as in my example in Unine (in which the point of no return for a decision made at noon is hit ten milliseconds before noon).

Let's stick just with deep openness for a while. Do we have evidence that it exists? Some people say it's obvious that we do. When we're unsure about what to do and mulling the matter over, it feels like more than one decision is open to us. But what would it feel like if, in fact, alternative decisions *weren't* open to us in the way deep openness requires? And what would it feel like if determinism is true of our universe?

The answer, as far as I can see, is this: just the way things normally feel. I'm not saying that we don't have deep openness. What I'm saying is that the difference between deep openness and its absence isn't the kind of thing that can be felt. We sometimes do feel uncertain about what we will do. But we can have exactly that feeling even if our universe is deterministic. Your not knowing what you will decide is one thing; having deep openness regarding what you will decide is another. And the same goes for deep-ish openness.

Many people can't taste the difference between Coke and Pepsi. And, as I see it, no one can *feel* the difference between deep (or deep-ish) openness and its absence. Of course, there are other ways for us to get evidence about whether a cola someone poured for us is Coke or Pepsi (or something else). And there may be ways, at least in principle, to get evidence about whether we have or lack deep openness. I'm certainly not saying that it's impossible for scientists ever to discover whether deep (or deep-ish) openness exists. My claim is only that the discovery won't be made by attending to how things feel to us.

So is there hard evidence of deep (or deep-ish) openness? In chapter 4, I mentioned some research on indeterminism in fruit flies that allegedly provides such evidence. Take an enormous leap from tiny animals to the entire universe. According to some interpretations of quantum mechanics, genuine chance is built into the fabric of the universe. If a certain photon veered left a moment ago and time were wound backward a couple of moments, that photon might veer right in the "replay." For all we know, the universe and our brains leave room for deep openness.

Someone might think the neuroscience experiments we examined in chapter 8 prove that the brain works deterministically—that there's no room in it for deep openness and no room for deep-ish openness. But, of course, they don't prove this. In these experiments, even the most impressive success rate at predicting what participants would do on the basis of brain readings was 80 percent. Here we have probabilities. So we have something compatible with the brain *not* working deterministically—with there being some wiggle room in the brain.

One more time. Is there hard evidence that our brains work indeterministically in the way they'd need to if we have deep openness? Is there evidence that sometimes, right up to the moment of decision, there really are different possibilities for what happens next in the brain—possibilities consistent with the way the universe was at some past time together with the laws of nature? Human brains are enormously complicated. It would be extremely difficult—and certainly not possible today—to control everything so you could tell that a brain event wasn't determined by anything and was partly a matter of chance. It's difficult (if not impossible) to do this even with fruit flies.

In light of these points about evidence, I'm not in a position to claim that free will, as characterized in a Mixed way, exists. But I'm in no position to claim that it doesn't exist either. The jury is still out on that. Even so, I can feel pretty good about the bottom line in my position on free will. Here's the bottom line again, but in a shortened form: The claim that free will doesn't exist is less credible than the claim that it does exist as conceived either in a Straight way or in a Mixed way.

3. Conclusion

Perhaps many readers of a book on free will would like to see the author make such bold claims as *Free will definitely exists* or *Free will is indisputably an illusion*. I can't, in good faith, make such claims myself. If I were convinced that compatibilism is true, I would confidently assert that free will exists, for reasons I mentioned in this chapter. The pro-free-will position that I have endorsed here is more cautious. But it is my position; it's a position I can—and do—sincerely endorse.

I knew that I would eventually arrive at a bottom line in this book. After all, an opinionated guide to free will has to voice an opinion on the topic. But arriving at a bottom line hasn't been the goal of this book. Instead, my aim has been to take you on a philosophical journey that would give you a good feel for the interesting issues, options, and arguments that need to be dealt with in any respectable attempt to arrive at a bottom line on free will, thereby helping you to think things through for yourself. I hope you enjoyed the tour.

REFERENCES

Beebee, H. 2013. *Free Will: An Introduction*. Houndmills: Palgrave Macmillan.

Bourget, D. and D. Chalmers, 2014. "What Do Philosophers Believe?" *Philosophical Studies* 170: 465–500.

Cashmore, A. 2010. "The Lucretian Swerve: The Biological Basis of Human Behavior and the Criminal Justice System." *Proceedings of the National Academy of Sciences of the United States of America* 107: 4499–504.

Frankfurt, H. 1969. "Alternate Possibilities and Moral Responsibility." *Journal of Philosophy* 66: 829–39.

Fried, I., R. Mukamel, and G. Kreiman. 2011. "Internally Generated Preactivation of Single Neurons in Human Medial Frontal Cortex Predicts Volition." *Neuron* 69: 548–562.

Gazzaniga, M. 2011. *Who's in Charge? Free Will and the Science of the Brain*. New York: HarperCollins.

Haggard, P., A. Mele, T. O'Connor, and K. Vohs. 2015. "Free Will Lexicon." In A. Mele, ed. *Surrounding Free Will*. New York: Oxford University Press, 319–26.

Harris, S. 2012. *Free Will*. New York: Free Press.

Libet, B. 1985. "Unconscious Cerebral Initiative and the Role of Conscious Will in Voluntary Action." *Behavioral and Brain Sciences* 8: 529–66.

Libet, B. 2001. "Consciousness, Free Action and the Brain." *Journal of Consciousness Studies* 8: 59–65.

Libet, B. 2004. *Mind Time*. Cambridge, MA: Harvard University Press.

Maoz, U., G. Yaffe, C. Koch, and L. Mudrik. 2019. "Neural Precursors of Decisions that Matter—an ERP Study of Deliberate and Arbitrary Choice." *eLife* 2019; 8:e39787.

Mele, A. 2006. *Free Will and Luck*. New York: Oxford University Press.

Mele, A. 2009. *Effective Intentions*. New York: Oxford University Press.

Mele, A. 2012. "Another Scientific Threat to Free Will?" *Monist* 95: 422–40.

Mele, A. 2014. *Free: Why Science Hasn't Disproved Free Will*. New York: Oxford University Press.

Mele, A. 2017. *Aspects of Agency*. New York: Oxford University Press.

Mele, A. 2019. *Manipulated Agents*. New York: Oxford University Press.

Mele, A. and D. Robb. 1998. "Rescuing Frankfurt-Style Cases." *Philosophical Review* 107: 97–112.

Montague, P. R. 2008. "Free Will." *Current Biology* 18: R584–85.

Ramachandran, V. 2004. *A Brief Tour of Human Consciousness*. New York: Pi Press.

Schultze-Kraft, M., D. Birman, M. Rusconi, C. Allefeld, K. Görgen, S. Dähne, B. Blankertz, and J. Haynes. 2016. "The Point of No Return in Vetoing Self-Initiated Movements." *Proceedings of the National Academy of Sciences* 113: 1080–85.

Soon, C., M. Brass, H. Heinze, and J. Haynes. 2008. "Unconscious Determinants of Free Decisions in the Human Brain." *Nature Neuroscience* 11: 543–45.

Stapp, H. 2007. *Mindful Universe*. Berlin: Springer.

Strawson, G. 2002. "The Bounds of Freedom." In R. Kane, ed. *The Oxford Handbook of Free Will*. New York: Oxford University Press.

Trevena, J. and J. Miller. 2010. "Brain Preparation before a Voluntary Action: Evidence against Unconscious Movement Initiation." *Consciousness and Cognition* 19: 447–56.

van Inwagen, P. 1983. *An Essay on Free Will*. Oxford: Clarendon Press.

Vonasch, A., R. Baumeister, and A. Mele. 2018. "Ordinary People Think Free Will Is a Lack of Constraint, Not the Presence of a Soul." *Consciousness and Cognition* 60: 133–51.

INDEX

For the benefit of digital users, indexed terms that span two pages (e.g., 52–53) may, on occasion, appear on only one of those pages.